FOOTBALL SKILLS

FOR YOUNG PLAYERS

TED BUXTON
WITH ALEX LEITH
AND JIM DREWITT

FOREWORD BY
GORDON JAGO

Grange
BOOKS

A QUANTUM BOOK

Produced by
Quantum Publishing Ltd
6 Blundell Street
London N7 9BH

This edition printed 2008

Published by Grange Books
an imprint of Grange Books Ltd.
35, Riverside
Sir Thomas Longley Road
Medway City Estate, Rochester
Kent ME2 4DP
www.grangebooks.co.uk

ISBN 978-1-84804-017-5

QUMSCDR

Manufactured in Hong Kong by
Regent Publishing Services Ltd
Printed in Singapore by
Star Standard Industries (Pte) Ltd

Picture Credits
l = left, r = right, t = top, b = bottom

Allsport: Front cover image of David Beckham – Ben Radford, inset image of Tiffeny Milbrett – Al Bello. Pp1
Ben Radford, 2-3 Ross Kinnaird, 5 Vincent Laforet, 21 Ben Radford, 23l Laurence Griffiths, 24b David Cannon,
25b Jed Jacobsohn, 26b Clive Brunskill, 27r Chris Lobina, 28b Ben Radford, 31r Mike Hewitt, 37 Ben Radford,
43 Ezra Shaw, 45 Stu Forster, 49 Ross Kinnaird, 50r Christophe Guibbaud, 53b Laurent Zabulon, 54 Stu Forster,
56-57 Shaun Botterill, 58 Alex Livesey, 61l Clive Brunskill, 63r Claudio Villa, 66t Ross Kinnaird, 68 Laurence
Griffiths, 73t Mike Hewitt, 75 Clive Brunskill, 78t Jed Jacobsohn, 79tl Caludio Villa, bl Tony O'Brien, tr Clive
Brunskill, br Jamie McDonald, 83b Clive Brunskill, 85 Gary M Prior, 86tr David Cannon, 88r Shaun Botterill,
89t Shaun Botterill, 89b Ben Radford, 90l Gary Palmer, 96t Craig Prentis, 99 Clive Brunskill, 100t Stu Forster,
102r Gary M Prior, 105b Alex Livesey, 109r Mike Hewitt, 111b Graham Chadwick, 113 Claudio Villa, 114r Stu
Forster, 117b Clive Brunskill, 119 Claudio Villa, 121t Stu Forster, b Vincent Laforet, 122 Ross Kinnaird, 125 Ben
Radford.

Contents

FOREWORD

BY GORDON JAGO

Professional teams spend hours preparing for every match because they know that they can improve their standard of play through practice, practice, and more practice. If you want to be a successful player, whether you play soccer with friends, are part of an amateur team, or aspire to become a professional, you need to follow this example. The skills that are developed during practice should enable you to play without having to think about what your feet are doing; it should become second nature.

This book, written by Ted Buxton, a former colleague of mine and a man of vast international soccer experience, sets out drills the professionals use to sharpen their skills. Some drills are simple, enabling you to master the basic skills needed to play well; others are more complex with diverse passing movements, and often involve the whole team. In short, there is something for everyone — young players, older players, and coaches, too.

As well as detailing skills and drills, advice is given on warming up and cooling down, vital processes in order to decrease the risk of injury and to increase suppleness. There are also general guidelines on what to eat and drink, pre-match for example, so that every player can maximize their own fitness and ability.

This book demonstrates that the key to successful training and playing is enjoyment. It is important not to slip into the sort of win-at-all-costs mentality that has become such a part of the professional game. Participation is the main thing. That said, winning is a pleasurable sensation for any player, and if these drills are practiced and the basic skills perfected, there is no doubt that you'll feel more confident in game situations and have more chance of being a winner.

Following a successful playing and coaching career in England, Gordon Jago went to live and work in the United States. He was the coach of the Tampa Bay Rowdies and is currently with the Dallas Sidekicks.

WARMING UP
AND STRETCHING

It is essential before any training session or match that the whole team warm up and then stretch in order to prepare their bodies for the coming action. Starting a match "cold" makes players unable to move as freely or quickly as they should and drastically increases the chances of pulling or straining a muscle. Muscle and tendon pulls account for over half of soccer injuries and this figure can be kept to a minimum if a full stretching routine is followed. Stretching also increases your stride length, so you run faster and farther. It helps maneuverability, too, aiding the ability to twist and turn. The older players get, the more important stretching and warm-up becomes — though this doesn't mean that younger players can avoid doing it.

It is vital to stretch all the major muscles to make them more supple and ready for the strain they are about to encounter in the coming training session or match. Before stretching it is important that the body be warm. Each stretch should be moved into and out of slowly. Never bounce on a stretch. It is important to remember to breathe out when moving into a stretch and ease out of a stretch if it becomes uncomfortable and the muscle begins to shake or burn.

Warm-up routine

Before starting on stretching routines you should do a gentle warm-up to increase your heart rate and get the blood pumping throughout your body, particularly in colder countries or seasons. This should incorporate a five-minute session of light jogging. Before a match it's a good idea for the team to do this together in a line. It will increase camaraderie and can dishearten the other team, who will see that you work as a unit even before the game. While running, swing the arms, elbows out, again in unison to create the same image of unity. Even singing a team song at this point is not out of the question.

General tips

You should be careful when stretching because getting it wrong can cause the kind of injuries you are trying to avoid. Here are some tips to safe and effective stretching:

• Never stretch until the body is warmed up
• Move in and out of each stretch slowly
• Hold each stretch in the furthest comfortable position (without causing any pain)
• Hold each stretch for about 10 to 20 seconds, keeping your body steady all the time. Count the seconds out, don't just guess
• Never bounce on the stretch
• Breathe out as you move into the stretch
• Never force a stretch so that it feels uncomfortable
• If the area being stretched does begin to feel uncomfortable, hurt, or shake, then ease back immediately
• Establish a consistent stretching routine. A regular pattern is believed by some to be better for your body and also helps ensure you don't forget a stretch
• Stretch both before and after exercise

LOWER-BODY STRETCHES

Hamstring stretch

Kneel on the ground stretching one leg out in front of you, with the heel on the ground and the toe pointing in the air. Put a little weight on the heel until you feel a gentle tension in the hamstring (which runs down the back of the thigh). Never jerk the muscles or tendons when stretching. Gently ease into the stretch and hold it for 20 seconds before easing off. Do this three times and change to the other leg.

Pelican thigh stretch

Stand on one leg, holding the foot of the other leg behind the buttocks with one hand. Your knees should be together, the supporting leg slightly bent, and your hips pressed forward. It is difficult to keep a sense of balance like this so use the other hand to balance against a tree or wall, or even a teammate. Ease the foot back slowly and feel the thigh muscles stretching. Ease into a full stretch for 20 seconds or so, then ease out again. Do this three times and change legs.

Groin stretch

Sit on your buttocks with the soles of your feet together, knees bent, pointing away from you. Using your elbows, gently press your knees downward to that you feel a stretch in the groin. Gently ease into the stretch, hold for 20 seconds, and ease out again. Do this three times.

Calf stretch

Put the weight of the body on the front foot, bending the knee and stretching the other leg behind, with the weight resting on the toes. Lean forward so your hands touch the ground. Point your feet forward — they should be parallel. Slowly lean forward and push the outstretched leg back slowly, feeling the calf muscle gently stretching. Gently ease into the stretch for 20 seconds and ease out. Repeat three times on each leg.

▲ Calf

▲ Hamstring   ▲ Pelican Thigh   ▲ Groin

▼ Total Body

▲ Bunny Hops

▲ Sit-up

UPPER-BODY STRETCHES

It's particularly important for goalkeepers to do upper-body stretching, but it's also important for outfield players. The upper body is used in various outfield activities such as jumping, and heading and throwing the ball, so do not neglect these stretches!

For upper body stretching, you should stand with your feet hip-width apart, knees slightly bent, and hips pressed forward. This is to prevent your lower back from arching.

Shoulder and side stretch

Stand straight with your legs slightly apart and knees slightly bent. Position your hands behind the head. Move the head down toward the side — feel the shoulders and side stretching. Hold for ten seconds, do three times, and change sides.

Arm and shoulder stretch

Hold your arms above your head, intertwining the fingers so the backs of the hands are above the head. Move your fingers upward until the shoulder muscles and the muscles in the arm stretch. Hold for ten seconds. Do this three times.

Shoulder stretch

Interlink your fingers behind your back so the palms are facing your back. Pull the fingers downward. Feel the muscles around the shoulder blades being stretched. Hold for ten seconds, and repeat three times.

Sideways neck stretch

Standing with your hands on your hips, put your head to one side so that your ear is nearer to your shoulder. Feel the muscles in the side of the neck begin to stretch. Hold for a count of five and ease out. Change and repeat on the other side. Then let your head drop back and raise the face upward, hold for a count of five, and return to an upright position. Drop the chin to the chest, hold for a count of five, and return to an upright position. Repeat this routine three times.

Pectoral stretch

A very simple move. Stand with your arms outstretched, gently press them backward. Hold the stretch for 20 seconds and release.

Upper back stretch

Lace your fingers together in front of your chest, with your palms facing you. Relax your shoulders and press your arms straight out in front of you. Feel the stretch ease through the upper back. Repeat three times.

Tricep stretch

Put your right leg forward, bending the knee, and stretch your left leg out behind you. Bend your left arm and pull it back slightly so that your fist rests at waist height. From this position straighten your arm; you should feel the muscle, in the back of your arm at the top, working. Repeat eight times. Only move the arm from the elbow not from the shoulder. When you change to your right arm, change your stance so that your left foot is forward.

▲ Pectoral

▲ Side and neck

▲ Waist

▲ Upper back　　　　　▲ Tricep　　　　　▲ Shoulder and upper arm

WARMING UP AND STRECHING 11

COOLING DOWN

It's as important to cool down after training sessions and matches as it is to warm up before them. Soccer is an extremely strenuous game, and simply stopping at the end of a game can lead to several problems:

- The excess lactic acid in your body after strenuous exercise can lead to restlessness and lack of sleep when rest and sleep are the very things you need to fully recover;
- The waste products built up in your body can lead to stiffness and aches in your muscles and joints for several days after the game, limiting your physical capacity;
- Rapid decrease in blood pressure, body temperature, and heart rate is potentially harmful to your health.

Players who do not cool down (as well as players who do not warm up) properly will be more prone to injury and less effective when doing physical exercise after the game. Their playing career is also likely to be shorter.

Cool down and stretch

All these problems can be alleviated by following a simple cool-down process, which is similar to the warm-up dealt with at the start – two minutes of gentle jogging then five minutes of stretches. Gently working out the major muscles will serve to eliminate waste products through the lymphatic system.

The body will release hormones that counteract the adrenaline produced during exercise, helping you to rest. And the gentle nature of the cool-down will mean that your heart rate, blood pressure, and body temperature will decrease gradually rather than suddenly.

Rehydration

It is also important that you rehydrate after a game. You may have lost up to 7 pints (4 liters) of water from your body through sweating and it is important to replace it. Isotonic drinks will help you to rehydrate more quickly than water — for isotonic drink recipes see page 18.

Stock up

After rehydrating make sure that you eat, in order to help stock up on carbohydrates — any meals rich in rice, bread, or pasta — which will replace the energy you have used up. Most pro clubs have a cafeteria in the training center for their players and offer these sorts of foods in abundance.

Rest

Make sure that you have a good night's sleep after exercise to enable your body to fully recuperate for the next day. Seven to eight hours is recommended, but this will vary according to need.

OFF-SEASON TRAINING

While the general level of training in the off-season does not need to be as intense as it is when you are playing every week, you will drastically notice the difference in your performance if you return to training for the new season having at least maintained basic levels of fitness. While it is good for the body to have a rest from the rigors of the game, a routine which includes running and some basic sprinting, possibly combined with some weight work and always with stretching, can mean the difference between making the team for the first game of the season or sitting it out on the substitute's bench.

Running

For players who already have a good level of fitness, regular (every two or three days) 3-mile (5-kilometer) runs during the off-season are excellent for maintaining fitness. When running for fitness the idea really is to run, not jog, and 3 miles (5 kilometers) is the optimum distance for soccer as anything else diminishes the power needed to play the game.

Sprinting

As well as running, you can maintain your fitness levels with an off-season sprint program, the aim being to establish a base of endurance and stamina to build on when full training resumes. For the body to recover, sprinting should be done no more than twice a week. The program (shown below) is designed for generally fit players who are serious about their soccer (and over 18 years old). It can be down-scaled to suit all levels although it should not be undertaken by anyone under the age of 11.

PRE-SEASON TRAINING ROUTINES

It is hugely important for teams to be fit at the start of the season, which is why professional clubs get their players back from the off-season two months or so before their first competitive match. Even though most will have continued to exercise during the break to stay in shape, they will still need to work hard to get back to full match fitness. A good pre-season training routine will make the team ready for action, right from the first kick-off. As a player, you need a combination of training that involves a mix of running, weight training, endurance work, flexibility development, and rest.

Running

At the very start of your team's pre-season training session it is important for you to build up fitness and stamina by doing some running. You should run every day, at first gently, then more strenuously. It is a good idea to break up long-distance runs with short, hard sprints to build up the kind of fitness needed for soccer. An ideal exercise would be for you to do a 4-mile (6-kilometer) run but with speed runs of 25, 55, and 80 yards (25, 50, and 75 meters) interspersed every 1,000 yards (915 meters). It is also possible for a coach to make the training more interesting by timing players and encouraging them to beat yesterday's time.

SPRINTING PROGRAM

Distance	Rest time between sprints	Distance	Rest time between sprints	Distance	Rest time between sprints
Week 1 to 2		**Week 3 to 4**		**Week 5 to 6**	
10 x 12 meters (13 yards)	30 seconds	10 x 18 meters (20 yards)	20 seconds	10 x 20 meters (22 yards)	20 seconds
20 x 12 meters (13 yards)	40 seconds	20 x 18 meters (20 yards)	30 seconds	20 x 25 meters (27 yards)	30 seconds
30 x 8 meters (9 yards)	1 minute	30 x 12 meters (13 yards)	45 seconds	30 x 18 meters (20 yards)	45 seconds
40 x 5 meters (6 yards)	1 minute	40 x 10 meters (11 yards)	1 minute	40 x 15 meters (16½ yards)	1 minute
50 x 3 meters (3 yards)		50 x 6 meters (6½ yards)		50 x 10 meters (11 yards)	

DRILL 1
SPRINT AND JOG

Purpose: to build up and improve sprinting strength, speed, stamina, and endurance
Players: 1 to whole squad
Level: all
Equipment: none

The players line up on the goalline, sprint to the six-yard box, and jog back. Then they jog to a line level with the penalty spot, 12 yards (11 meters) out, and sprint back at full speed. Next they jog to the edge of the penalty area (18 yards/ 16 meters) and sprint back, again at full speed. Finally, they jog to the edge of the center circle and run back at three-quarter speed. At the beginning of pre-season training you should take two minutes to recover, then repeat the exercise. As you get closer to the start of the season, this time should be reduced until eventually you should be able to complete the exercise with just 15 seconds recovery time.

As you get fitter, it is possible to increase the number of times you have to perform the drill, or add a "pyramid" effect, which means you have to jog to and sprint back from the six-yard box four times, the penalty spot three times, the edge of the box twice, and the center circle once.

Again, start by taking three minutes to recover before repeating this exercise, reducing that to 30 seconds as the season approaches.

To add a competitive edge and to encourage a feeling of team spirit, the drill can be done as a relay, pitting two teams against each other and/or against the clock.

DRILL 2
FOLLOW MY LEADER

Purpose: to work on short-sprint speed and stamina and to build and improve general fitness
Players: 3 to 5
Level: all
Equipment: none

A line of three to five players begin jogging around a perimeter, with a gap of 3 yards (3 meters) between each of them. On the command of a coach or a designated player, the player at the back of the line has to run at three-quarter striding speed to the front of the line, and start leading the group. This should be repeated every 30 seconds. Initially this drill can be done for five minutes or so, with the duration being increased as the new season approaches.

Track events

In the final two weeks before the start of the season, once the players' speed and endurance is back up to an optimum level, introduce running races. The players can compete over 100 and 800 yards (90 and 730 meters). Each individual player should be timed during every race they run. If players are competitive, they will enjoy a training routine more, however grueling it may seem, and if they are made aware that their times are improving it will make it seem worthwhile.

QUICK FEET

Purpose: to build up stamina in the legs and to work on sharpness and agility
Players: 1 to whole squad
Level: all
Equipment: 10 to 20 marker cones

This exercise helps sharpen up your footwork coordination and balance. It encourages sharpness, speed, and accuracy — skills that are needed when you start to practice with a ball.

Set up a line of cones in a zigzag formation. Each player should "dance" through the cones, making sure they don't step on or knock over any.

Gym work
You can supplement your pre-season training routines with trips to the gym. General playing and training will naturally strengthen your lower body, but upper body strength is also crucial in soccer for balance, holding other players off, and challenging for the ball. If you want to undertake gym work you should always seek advice from a professional instructor who will design a personal program for you, based on your size, strength, and fitness.

Ball work
At this stage it's important to pay attention to ball work. Pick some of the simpler exercises from this book (especially from pages 22 to 35). You will need to reacquaint yourself with the ball to recover and improve your mastery of it. It is best to do ball work sessions before energy-sapping runs and endurance exercises as, if attempted afterward, player fatigue (mental and physical) will render them ineffective.

Games
Soccer players love playing soccer and no training session should ever be completed without at least a short game, whether it be five-, seven-, or eleven-a-side. It is also important in the pre-season period to organize a series of friendly 11-a-side games, so the coach can assess the form of each player individually and the team as a whole, and so that players can regain their match fitness. Of course, you should take into account the standard of the opposition (a huge defeat would not boost your team's spirit) and the timing of any match in regard to the rest of the pre-season training.

DIET

In order to be fit for the new season, it is important to plan your diet carefully and to make sure the plan is put into practice. The key to a diet for both health and sports performance is balance. If you need to lose weight (carrying too much body fat can affect your performance) you should reduce the amount of fat in your diet. However, you should not cut out fat completely.

Providing enough of the right sort of fuel for exercise (carbohydrate) will help to get the most out of training sessions and help to prevent fatigue toward the end of a match. Make sure the diet contains enough protein. Correct training and the supporting diet are the only ways to increase muscle mass. The diet must also provide all the essential nutrients such as vitamins and minerals for overall fitness and health.

Soccer players should try to have a diet that provides at least 55% of total energy as carbohydrate, 15% of total energy as protein, and the remainder as fat.

Cutting back on fats

Cutting back on fats helps you to get in shape for the new season. Here are some suggestions on how to do it:
• Use a low-fat margarine instead of butter, but spread it thinly.
• Switch to 1% or 2% milk.
• Keep creamy sauces to a minimum. Use tomato-based sauces or melted low-fat soft cheese instead.
• Light or oil-free dressings are better choices than mayonnaise or creamy dressings.
• Lean red meat, skin-free chicken, and fish are good sources of low-fat, protein-rich foods.
• Keep fried foods and sweets to a minimum.

Vegetarians

A well-planned diet that does not contain meat, fish, or poultry can provide all of the nutrients and energy that a soccer player needs.
• Include a wide variety of vegetarian sources of protein
• Use low-fat dairy foods as a regular part of your diet
• Maintain a good iron intake by including plenty of whole-grain cereals, whole-wheat bread, legumes (peas, beans etc.), green vegetables, and fortified breakfast cereals.
• Improve the absorption of iron by having vitamin-C rich foods at the same time, for example fruit, fruit juice, vegetables.

Sources of protein

Proteins are needed for growth and repair of the body. They make up part of the structure of all the cells in the body, particularly those that make up muscle tissue. Proteins are obtained from animal and vegetable sources. Listed below are sources of dietary protein.

Animal sources

• Beef, lamb, and pork—lean cuts
• Liver and kidney
• Lean ham and bacon
• Poultry
• Fish
• Milk, cheese, yogurt, eggs
• Always use low-fat choices where possible — 1% or 2% milk, low-fat yogurt, and low- or reduced- fat cheeses.)

If you are participating in vigorous activity on a regular basis, such as playing soccer and running, you are burning fat at a high rate. Don't obsess about how much fat you consume; it's more important that you eat healthy foods in the amounts that your body requires to maintain your lifestyle — no more, no less. If you have concerns about what you are eating, talk with your doctor or school nurse.

Vegetable sources
- Beans — baked, red kidney etc.
- Peas, lentils, and other legumes
- Nuts and seeds
- Bread, potatoes, rice, pasta, cereals

Soya products
- Although not particularly high in protein, the amount eaten to meet the carbohydrate requirement will "incidently" make a significant contribution to protein intake as well.

A good diet provides the energy needed to prevent fatigue setting in toward the end of long, hard training sessions. It helps to keep the body well hydrated before, during, and after every training session and refuels the exercised muscles. You should always drink at least two large glasses of water before training and playing.

Refueling
You need to refuel as soon as possible after every training session — ideally within the first 30 minutes and certainly within an hour of finishing the session.
- High-carbohydrate, low-fat snacks and isotonic sports drinks are good choices.
- Make sure you keep up a high-carbohydrate intake throughout the day.
- Don't skip meals — it is much harder, if not impossible, to meet your energy requirements.
- If a training session is in the morning, don't skip breakfast for another half-hour in bed. Fuel levels need to be topped up after the "fast" of the night.
- Make sure every meal is based on a good source of carbohydrates.

Snacks for refueling
- Bananas
- Dried fruit — apricots, raisins for instance
- Granola or protein bars
- Pancakes
- Low-fat whole-grain muffins or rolls
- Low-fat crackers
- Isotonic sports drinks

Good sources of carbohydrates
- Breakfast cereals, whole-grain preferred
- Breads, muffins, bagels, and similar, whole-grain preferred
- Pasta and noodles
- Rice
- Baked beans
- Potatoes — mainly boiled, mashed, or baked
- Pizzas — but watch the high-fat toppings such as extra cheese and pepperoni
- Fruits and vegetables such as carrots, celery
- Yogurt with fresh fruit
- Fruit juice, unsweetened

What to drink
When sweat losses are small, water is fine. But as soon as the sweat rate increases (because of training intensity, warm weather, or high humidity) a drink that contains water, some carbohydrate and some sodium is a better choice. This helps to keep the body hydrated and also tops up the fuel level as well. These drinks can be bought in the store or made. Here are some possibilities.
- Sports drinks that contain up to 8 % carbohydrate (no more than 7 grams per 100 milliliters/¼ pint)
- 2 ounces (50 grams) of glucose or sugar, large pinch of salt to make 2 pints (1 liter) with water
- 1 pint (500 milliliters) of unsweetened orange or grapefruit juice, large pinch of salt and 1 pint (500 milliliters) of water
- ½ pint (200 milliliters) of soda pop (not diet) and a large pinch of salt to make about 2¼ pints (1.3 liters) with water.

Make up a new batch of drink every day and throw away any unused drink. Remember to keep your water bottle very clean. Sugary drinks attract bugs and other nasty things. This is important at all times, but especially during warm weather.

USING THE BOOK

The following chapters contain a series of drills that will help you learn the basics of the game if you are a beginner, or if you already have some playing experience the drills will help you build upon what you have already learned. In addition to the drills there are skill boxes, which teach you the essential elements of the game — kicking the ball, passing, shooting — these skills are then practiced in the drills. The purpose of the drill is clearly explained, along with how many players are involved, what equipment is needed, and what skill level players doing the drill should be at.

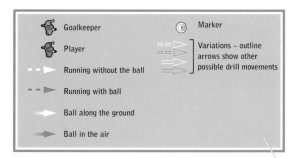

Goalkeeper

Player

Running without the ball

Running with ball

Ball along the ground

Ball in the air

Marker

Variations – outline arrows show other possible drill movements

Skill levels

Beginner
Players in their first year of playing soccer at an organized level. These drills will help you practice the skills of trapping and passing the ball, basic heading, and shooting. Once these have been mastered, players can then move on to the next level.

Intermediate
Players who have mastered the basic skills but who need to keep working on them so that they become second nature. These players can then move on to more difficult skills. Intermediate players should be aware of basic tactics and have a good level of fitness. Only through playing and training regularly for some years will intermediate players become advanced ones.

Advanced
Players who have a high level of natural ability, coupled with several years of experience of playing the game and receiving good coaching. Advanced players are highly skilled and tactically aware.

Each drill has a number and title, and the essential information of the purpose of the drill, the number of players involved, the skill level, and the equipment needed are detailed.

These boxes detail the essential skills of the game.

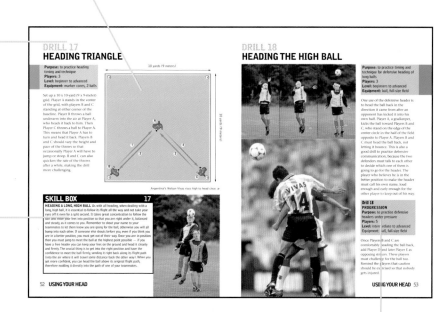

Many of the drills have progressions, which test your abilities that little bit further.

chapter one

BALL WORK BASICS

It doesn't matter how gifted you are at soccer, if you haven't spent hours and hours practicing your ball work your ball skills will not be as good as they could be. Practicing skills with the ball is a vital part of match preparation for a seasoned professional or a beginner.

It is important for you to be comfortable with the ball. You should be able to kick it in a number of different ways, control it at whatever height and pace it comes to you, and have the ability to dribble it at speed.

Match practice and training practice helps hone these skills, but practicing ball work is necessary for improvement. The more practice you put in, the more able you'll be to get the ball to do exactly what you want, using the head, the feet, the knees, or any other part of the body (apart, of course, from the hands and arms).

The following section details drills that can be carried out to help improve these essential skills. Some are designed for the individual, others are for small groups of players, or even a whole team. Remember, practice makes perfect and permanent.

RONALDO

The Brazilian striker Ronaldo is one of the most skillful players in the game. His ability to achieve the unexpected with the ball has made him the scourge of defenders the world over. Ronaldo is an exceptionally gifted player, but his mastery of the ball could not have been achieved without hours and hours of practice.

DRILL 4
WALLBALL

The England team manager and former player Kevin Keegan recalls that as a youngster he spent much of his free time kicking a ball against a wall in his street, and most professional players will be able to relate a similar experience. Wallball incorporates the two most essential elements of soccer — kicking and controlling — and can be of as much use to the more experienced player as to the beginner. The constant repetition requires great concentration.

Find a suitable wall (preferably one with no windows in it or anywhere nearby) high enough that the ball doesn't keep going over it. The ideal place is in a gym.

You should stand about 5 yards (5 meters) away from the wall and sidefoot the ball at its base (see Skill Boxes 1 and 2 on pages 23 and 24 for basic kicking styles). When it rebounds, you should control it

WALLBALL/THE SIDEFOOT

with the inside of your foot, trying to stop the ball dead by "trapping" it (see Skill Box 3 on page 25 on control). When the ball is under control — in other words, stopped dead at your feet — you should kick it back and start again. As you feel more comfortable, particularly with controlling the ball, you can kick it harder at the wall, making it come back more quickly and so making it harder to control. You can also switch to kicking and controlling with the weaker foot.

▼ Belgium's Giles de Bilde concentrates on getting it right.

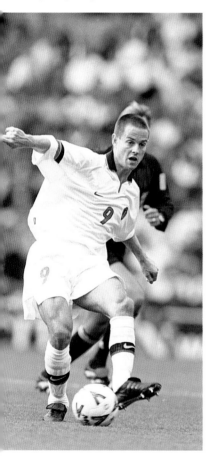

SKILL BOX   1

THE SIDEFOOT The sidefoot is used for short passes and is generally the most precise and accurate way to kick the ball. This is because the foot makes contact with a large part of the ball's surface area. As with all passing, kicking, and shooting in soccer it is vital to watch the ball at all times. Position your nonkicking foot 6 to 8 inches (15 to 20 centimeters) to the side of the ball (it should be facing the direction in which the ball is to be passed) and, with only a short backswing, bring your kicking leg forward at a right angle to the nonkicking leg and kick the ball with the inside of your foot. At the moment that the ball is kicked, lean forward over it, watching the ball at all times, and follow through with your kicking leg in the direction of the target.

BALL WORK BASICS
THE DRIVE

SKILL BOX 2

THE DRIVE The drive is used to get power into the kick, although it is harder to be as accurate with it as with the sidefoot. Your nonkicking foot should be placed alongside the ball, 6 to 8 inches (15 to 20 centimeters) away. Keep your kicking leg facing straight at the target and, using a full backswing and keeping your head, upper body, and knee over the ball, strike it using the instep (where the laces of the shoe are). Your foot should be extended so that its middle makes contact with the middle of the ball — if the ball is hit at the bottom, it will go into the air; if it is hit too near the top, the force of the kick will be lost into the ground. It is also crucial to keep your ankle rigid as the ball is struck, allowing the power from your leg to transfer directly to the ball.

▼ Poise and power from Thierry Henry of France.

PASSING/TRAPPING

SKILL BOX   3

TRAPPING THE BALL This is the skill of being able to instantly stop and control a ball that has been passed along the ground. This is a crucial skill because the quicker you can get the ball under control the more time you will have to decide what to do with it before opponents put you under pressure.

Directly face the oncoming ball, so that it is coming onto your kicking foot. Take up position to make a sidefoot pass, so that the ball comes onto the inside of the foot (making contact with the maximum surface area to kill the ball's speed). Watch it all the way onto your foot, and at the moment of impact bring your foot backward in the direction the ball is going — this will cushion the impact. If the foot is kept straight and the ball is simply allowed to hit it, it will bounce off and away from you. The purpose of trapping is to stop the ball dead at your feet, putting you instantly in control. The harder the ball is traveling at you the further back you should bring your foot and the faster you should move it. Remember to stay relaxed and confident, bending your knees and leaning over the ball. You can also trap and control the ball with the outside of your foot, this way you can trap and move in one movement.

DRILL 4
PROGRESSION A
Purpose: to practice accurate sidefoot passing and control
Players: 1
Level: beginner to advanced
Equipment: ball, 2 marker cones, wall

Stand 8 yards (7 meters) from the wall, in front of which you have placed two marker cones 1 yard (1 meter) apart. Standing directly in front of the cones you must sidefoot the ball between them so that it hits the wall and bounces back to you. When it does, trap it and start again.

◀ Julie Foudy gets the ball under control in the 1998 Women's World Cup final.

DRILL 4
WALLBALL

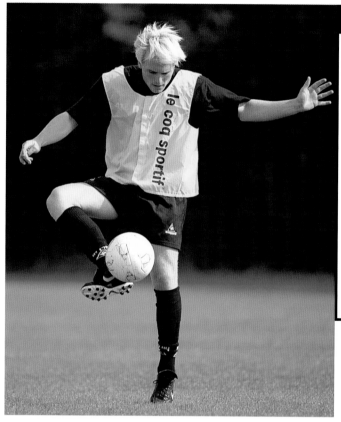

SKILL BOX 4

TRAPPING A HIGH BALL Sometimes the ball will not be passed conveniently along the ground, so you should be able to control it when it is delivered in the air, either directly or after bouncing. The same basic rules in Skill Box 3 (see page 25) apply, but obviously the kicking foot needs to be lifted off the ground to meet the ball. This means that it is especially crucial to determine the flight path of the ball and get into position early, so that when the kicking foot is raised you are well balanced and concentrating only on the ball. Watch the ball all the way onto the side of your foot, and, as it meets it, cushion the ball as before with your lower leg but keep your upper leg firm and solid. This will give you the strength to stop the ball and keep you balanced so that, as the ball drops at your feet, you have it under control and are poised to play it.

▼ Brazilian maestro Juninho traps the ball in an instant.

DRILL 4
PROGRESSION B
Purpose: to practice trapping a fast-moving ball
Players: 1
Level: beginner to advanced
Equipment: ball, wall

Stand 3 yards (3 meters) away from the wall and sidefoot the ball against it. Because you are so near it will bounce back to you hard and fast (exactly how fast depends on your initial kick), and you must stop it dead by trapping it. Once the ball is under control you can start again.

DRILL 4
PROGRESSION C
Purpose: to learn how to sidefoot a moving ball
Players: 1
Level: beginner to advanced
Equipment: ball, wall

Stand 4 yards (4 meters) away from the wall. Play a sidefoot pass against it, then when it rebounds you must sidefoot it back without "trapping" it first. You can repeat this movement over and over again, increasing the speed of your first pass so that returning it becomes harder and harder.

THE SIDEFOOT

SKILL BOX   5

SIDEFOOTING A MOVING BALL

Sometimes in a match you won't have time to control the ball before passing it because there will be opponents closing down on you, so you will have to kick a moving ball. The basics are the same as if the ball were not moving (see Skill Box 1 on page 23), but, instead of waiting for the ball to come onto your foot and then cushioning it, you must watch it very carefully and then bring your foot to meet it. You should angle your body so that you are in a position to receive the ball but you should also be facing the way you want to pass the ball. Anticipating the movement of the ball toward you and responding to it, play the pass exactly as described in Skill Box 1, but remember that, because the ball is already moving, you will not need as much backlift to get the same amount of power in the ball. Angle your foot in the direction of your target, meet the ball, and in one short, sharp movement send it on its way.

▲ Graham Alexander keeps his body balanced and his eyes on the ball.

BALL WORK BASICS
VOLLEYING

BASIC VOLLEYING Volleying a ball in the air takes concentration, balance, and good technique. Get in position early, so that when the ball comes onto your kicking foot you have plenty of room to strike it. As the ball comes to you, put your weight on the ball of your nonkicking foot, and raise the knee of your kicking foot in the air in anticipation. Watch the ball carefully and swing your foot at it, keeping your head down and your arms in the air for balance. Connect with the ball with your instep (the laced part of your shoe) and follow through. Don't worry too much about power: you don't need a full backlift, and it is more important to make good, clean contact. To ensure this, watch the ball all the way onto your foot, volleying with a smooth, steady action, keeping your head still and following through in the direction of the target.

DRILL 4
PROGRESSION D
Purpose: to establish basic volleying skills
Players: 2
Level: beginner to advanced
Equipment: 10 balls, wall

Player A stands 5 yards (5 meters) away from the wall. Player B stands 2 yards (2 meters) to one side of Player A (to the left or right) and throws the ball underarm at the wall — aiming for a point about 5 feet (2 meters) high. Practice the underarm throw first to get the ball coming back at the right height for volleying. This will depend on the size of the player doing the drill. Once the ball has been thrown, Player A must get into position and volley it back against the wall. The ball is likely to bounce past both players so it is best to have a number of balls, say 10. After all 10 have been used, collect them and then swap roles.

In the air or on the ground, it doesn't matter to Juninho. ▶

BALL WORK BASICS
HEADING

1 Anticipating the flight of the ball.
2 The point of contact.

SKILL BOX   7

BASIC HEADING Heading the ball is all about keeping your eye on the ball right up to the moment that you head it. Follow its flight as it comes toward you, moving your feet into position (so that you are underneath the ball as it comes to you, though ideally in a position that allows you to step forward to make contact) so that you can meet it firmly and cleanly without being off balance. When it comes to you, adjust your position so that you can meet it with your forehead. Keep watching the ball and tense your neck muscles at the moment of impact, nodding your head firmly forward to meet the ball and give added power to the play. Heading does *not* mean flinging your head at the ball, which can cause injury. You must see your head as the end point of an instrument — your whole body — and of that instrument's power. The head is not itself an instrument, keep this in mind every time you head the ball.

DRILL 4
PROGRESSION E
Purpose: to practice basic heading
Players: 2
Level: beginner to advanced
Equipment: 10 balls, wall

Player A stands 5 yards (5 meters) from the wall. Player B stands 2 yards (2 meters) to one side of Player A (to the left or right) and throws the ball underarm at the wall — aiming for a point about 5 feet (2 meters) high. The height of the throw depends upon the height of the player heading the ball. Practice the throw first to get it right. Player A must then get into position and head it back against the wall. The ball is likely to bounce past both players so it is best to have a number of balls at hand. After all 10 have been used, collect them and then the players should swap roles.

DRILL 5
ADVANCED TRAPPING

Purpose: to develop and practice ball control
Players: 2
Level: beginner to advanced
Equipment: ball

As we have already seen, trapping the ball is one of the essential skills of the game (see Skill Box 3 on page 25). Like all skills, even when it has been mastered it needs to be practiced over and over again to maintain eye–foot coordination and your skill level.

This drill is a simple but effective pairs routine. Player A passes the ball to Player B, who controls it with one touch and passes it back. You should vary the height and speed of the balls you play to each other, so you are not just trapping balls on the ground but also in the air. As well as the sidefoot trap, you can trap the ball with the soles of your feet (see Skill Box 8), with other parts of your feet, with your thighs, with your chest (see Skill Box 9), or even with your head. The important thing to remember when trapping the ball with any part of the body is to cushion the ball by making the impact as soft as possible so that it comes under control.

BALL CONTROL SKILLS

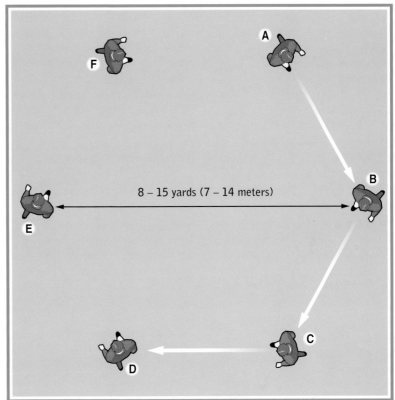

8 – 15 yards (7 – 14 meters)

DRILL 5
PROGRESSION
Purpose: further development of ball-control skills
Players: 2 to 6
Level: beginner to advanced
Equipment: ball

The basic drill can be varied by adding more players. Stand in a circle with a diameter of 8 to 15 yards (7 to 14 meters). The more players the bigger the circle. Now pass to each other as before.

The world's most famous player, ▶ Ronaldo, of Brazil, rarely loses control of the ball.

DRILL 6
JUGGLING

Purpose: to practice basic ball skills
Players: 1
Level: beginner to advanced
Equipment: ball

Juggling is the practice of keeping the ball in the air using the feet, thighs, head, chest, and shoulders. Basically it means keeping the ball off the ground and under control, using mainly the feet but also pretty much anywhere on the body apart from the arms and hands. Give a professional a ball and he will almost always start practicing juggling. Though rarely used in match situations, it is an essential part of basic training since it develops eye–foot coordination, general touch, and an all-around "feel" for the ball.

You should start practicing with your stronger foot. Drop the ball onto the foot and gently tap it into the air so that it doesn't fly away from the body and you are able to perform the action again (and hopefully again and again).

Try to put a little backspin on the ball (see Skill Box 10); since this will keep it close to the body and make it easier to control. If you've not attempted this before the ball will probably spin out of control pretty soon. Gradually you will learn to keep the ball under enough control to keep it in the air for some time. Record the number of times you and your fellow players touch the ball before it hits the ground and each player should try to beat their score the next time.

When you're able to keep the ball up five or six times you should start to incorporate your weaker foot into the play. Start trying to switch the ball from the right to the left foot and vice versa.

After a while you will be able to vary the height of the ball, and use your thighs as well to keep the ball up. Once you get really proficient, you will be able to incorporate your shoulders, chest, and head, too but never your arms and hands, of course.

SKILL BOX 10

PUTTING BACKSPIN ON THE BALL As the ball drops toward your foot, rather than keeping your foot flat and just kicking it back up, try to jab forward with a little stabbing movement at the bottom of the ball as you make contact. This will cause it to spin backward slightly, making it stay closer to your body and therefore easier to control.

SKILL BOX   11

SCOOPING THE BALL INTO THE AIR Experienced soccer players don't drop the ball onto their foot to juggle it. They roll their foot from the top of the ball around to the bottom, then scoop it up. This instantly adds backspin to the ball, making it easier to keep control. Learn to do this as soon as you start practicing juggling.

DRILL 6
JUGGLING

DRILL 6
PROGRESSION A
Purpose: further development of ball skills
Players: 2
Level: intermediate to advanced
Equipment: ball

Player A takes the ball and begins keeping it in the air with his feet. Then Player B (or the coach) shouts out instructions for him to follow such as "five below the knee" (five small kicks where the ball must not go higher than the knee); "five on the thigh" (the ball must be controlled on the thigh); "five on the head," and so on. The player must follow these instructions while keeping the ball in the air.

DRILL 6
PROGRESSION B
Purpose: further development of ball skills, bringing together controlling and volleying
Players: 2
Level: intermediate to advanced
Equipment: ball

Player A throws the ball at chest height to Player B. The throw is crucial: it should be underarm and not too hard. Player B controls the ball on his chest (see Skill Box 9 on page 30), lets it drop to his thigh, bounces the ball onto his foot, and volleys it back to Player A. Player B then throws the ball to Player A, who then repeats the exercise for his partner.

DRILL 6
PROGRESSION C

Purpose: polishing basic ball skills
Players: 1 to 6
Level: intermediate to advanced
Equipment: ball

Juggling in pairs or groups is a good way to help a team bond (and understand one another's limitations). If professionals arrive at training early they will often start juggling in pairs to get a "feel" for the ball and warm up. One player will kick the ball to another, who will juggle it a little before passing it back — still in the air. Players carry on as long as they can without letting the ball touch the ground.

If practicing in a pair, structure can be added to the drill by making each player go through a set routine (foot, knee, shoulder, head) before they pass the ball back, or they can be limited to one part of the body. This can be a valuable exercise for strengthening the weaker foot, or for getting players used to heading the ball.

If practicing in a group (of up to six people) variations can be applied. The coach or a designated player can shout out the name of the player who should receive the ball, or he can insist that players use only their weaker foot for a period of time. All of these variations make the exercise more demanding.

DRILL 6
PROGRESSION D

Purpose: to practice intermediate ball skills with a competitive edge
Players: 1 to 30
Level: intermediate to advanced
Equipment: 1 to 30 balls

Everybody in the squad is given a ball and, on the coach's/teammate's whistle, they are instructed to keep it up in the air for as long as possible. The last one left with the ball in motion wins. Alternatively, if there aren't enough balls to go around, time each member of the squad with a stopwatch.

chapter two

PASS MASTER

In the early days of modern soccer the game was all about dribbling and tackling. Then the Scottish invented the passing game and became pretty much unbeatable. Soon everyone else followed suit. The ability to move the ball up the field at speed from player to player has remained a key part of the game ever since. Quite simply, if a team can't pass accurately, they're not going to win.

Passing can be done with any part of the foot. The instep is generally used for a long ball, the inside of the foot for a safer, shorter pass. The outside of the shoe is often an effective method of curving a pass and surprising the opposition — a well-placed back-heel kick can completely deceive a defense. You can even pass with other parts of your body — your head is a vital tool, as is your chest.

Passing also enables a team to keep possession and it is worth emphasizing that a team cannot score if it does not have possession. A well-placed pass from midfield to a point in front of an attacker's run can set up a goal, and the ability to do passes like this is one of the most prized assets in the game. One much-maligned but very useful method of passing is the long ball. This can vary from an aimless "thump" up front by a beleaguered defender to an inch-perfect diagonal ball from a gifted midfielder.

Like any other aspect of the game, passing in all its various forms must be practiced before any player can be sure of being effective in a game.

DIDIER DESCHAMPS

The French midfield maestro Didier Deschamps is one of football's pass masters. A European Cup winner with the Italian giants Juventus and a World Cup winner with France, Deschamps plays in the center of midfield. From there he controls the play, stealing the ball and then bringing a teammate into the game with an accurate pass. Rarely will you see Deschamps playing a hopeful long ball into space; he always tries to pick out a teammate in a good position and then play the ball to him neatly, right to his feet. This means that his team invariably retains possession, and you can only hurt the opposition when you've got the ball.

DRILL 7
THE SIDEFOOT PASS

Purpose: to practice accurate sidefoot passing
Players: 2 to 6
Level: beginner to intermediate
Equipment: ball

The key to passing is accuracy, and the most accurate method of passing is the sidefoot pass (see Skill Box 1 on page 23). The best way to practice this is in pairs. If there is a group of six players, four of them can practice the drill while two rest, and they can then be swapped in, so all players have the opportunity for a short break.

Player A passes to Player B, who is standing 10 yards (9 meters) away. Player B controls the ball and passes back. The passes should be so accurate that the players hardly have to move (they should need to make only a slight alteration in their stance) to control them. After a successful pass they each take a step back and repeat the process, continuing until a pass is misplaced, at which point they start again at a distance of 10 yards (9 meters).

Drill 7
PROGRESSION A
Purpose: to develop the accuracy of the sidefoot pass
Players: 3
Level: beginner to intermediate
Equipment: ball

Three players stand in a triangle, 6 yards (5 meters) apart. They pass to each other, stepping back a pace after each series of successful passes to make the triangle (and so the distance between them) bigger.

PROGRESSION B
Purpose: to practice the sidefoot pass within a large group of players, encouraging awareness and control
Players: 6 to 10
Level: intermediate to advanced
Equipment: ball

The players stand in a circle (diameter 18 yards/16 meters). Player A starts with the ball and the coach or a designated player shouts out the name of another player to pass to. The process is repeated. When the team gets used to the drill, make it into a game whereby players are knocked out of the circle when they miss a pass.

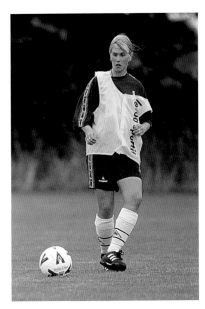

PASS AND RUN

Purpose: to practice accurate passing and control of a moving ball
Players: 2
Level: beginner to intermediate
Equipment: marker cones, ball

It is just as important for players to make themselves available for passes from other players as it is to play passes themselves. Moving off the ball is crucial in soccer. There's no point in having a team of good passers if there's never anyone free and able to receive the ball. This drill practices not just passing, but also running off the ball to receive a return.

Two players stand on the baseline of a 20 x 50-yard (18 x 46-meter) grid. Player A runs off and Player B passes the ball into his path, then immediately sprints off himself. A stops to receive and control the ball, waits until B is in front of him, then passes the ball into his path. Then he sprints forward. When the players reach the end of the grid, they turn around and start again.

SKILL BOX   12

PASSING TO A PLAYER ON THE RUN If you are passing to an open player who is moving into open space, it is crucial to play the ball in front of him. If you play it toward where his feet are at the moment you strike the ball, by the time the ball gets to him a second or so later it will be behind him. So play the ball *ahead* of the player on the move. The faster he is moving, the further ahead he will need the ball to be. Always try to play a ball so that the player receiving it will not have to break or adjust his stride pattern to receive the pass.

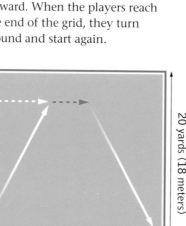

20 yards (18 meters)

50 yards (46 meters)

DRILL 9
HIT AND RUN

Purpose: to enhance passing skills and awareness when running off the ball
Players: 3
Level: beginner to advanced
Equipment: marker cones, ball

Three players line up in a 10 x 25-yard (9 x 23-meter) grid. Player A is on the baseline, players B and C are 10 yards (9 meters) ahead, with C 10 yards (9 meters) to the right of B. A passes to B, then makes a run behind C. B passes to C, then C collects the ball and passes to A, who has now arrived on his right. The players return to the baseline and swap roles.

When all three have made the run, the drill is altered so that C is standing to the left of B, and A has to make his run to the left. This drill can be altered to include different running and passing movements.

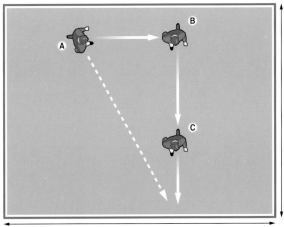

10 yards (9 meters)

25 yards (23 meters)

SKILL BOX 13

PASSING WITH THE OUTSIDE OF THE FOOT This play can be useful if you need to play a pass along or close to the ground with more power than a sidefoot pass (in other words, the ball needs to travel farther). You can also exert spin on the ball, making it "inswing." To execute a pass with the outside of the shoe, prepare as if to drive the ball (see Skill Box 2 on page 24), but, instead of hitting it in the middle with the laces of your shoe, hit it through the side with the outside of the shoe. Your body shape, stance, and head position should be exactly the same as when driving the ball.

DRILL 10
HITTING IT LONG

Purpose: to develop and practice playing accurate, lofted long balls
Players: 2
Level: intermediate to advanced
Equipment: ball

A game plan based entirely on long balls from the defense or midfield is suited to teams with athletic prowess and little skill. However, even the most able sides should be able to "mix it" or play occasional long balls to vary their attacking strategies. Accurate passes over 50 yards (46 meters) can enable quick forwards to get behind defenders and create one-on-one situations with the opposing goalkeeper from which they should score a goal.

So it is important to practice long passes, which are usually performed with the instep or the inside of the foot (see Skill Box 14 on page 43) as well as, on occasions, with the outside of the foot (see Skill Box 13 on page 41).

Player A stands 25 yards (23 meters) away from Player B, who hits the ball to his feet. Player B then passes the ball back to Player A. They both step back a couple of paces, and repeat the process, until they are 50 yards (46 meters) apart.

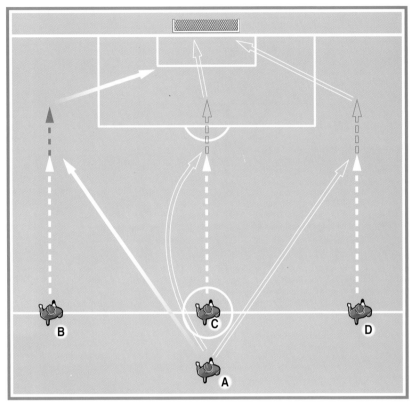

Purpose: to practice accurate long balls to teammates on the run
Players: 4 to 7
Level: intermediate to advanced
Equipment: ball, full-size field

Player A stands on the edge of the center circle. Players B, C, and D stand with their backs to him on the halfway line — B on the left wing, C on the center spot, D on the right wing. On a command from the coach or a designated player, they sprint toward the opposite goal. The coach/player then shouts out one of the names of the three players, and Player A must play a long pass into his path. He should receive the ball about 25 yards (23 meters) from goal. The move can be completed with a shot at goal, or a cross or pass to one of the other attackers.

Once the drill has been perfected in its basic form, three defenders can be brought in to make it more difficult.

◀ Dani of Portugal hits it long.

SKILL BOX   14

THE LONG PASS To get distance on your pass you need to loft the ball into the air, getting it to travel over other players' heads, also preventing it from being slowed down by contact with the field. To do this you must strike the bottom of the ball, following through and literally lifting it into the air. You will need to take a stride or two as you approach the ball, and because you also need to get your foot right under the ball it is best to approach at a slight angle (from the left if you are right-footed, from the right if you are left-footed). As you run up to the ball, plant your nonkicking foot about 8 inches (20 centimeters) to the side of the ball, keep your body over the ball and at the same time swing your kicking leg straight back. As you kick the ball — making contact with your instep — lean back slightly (the more you lean back the higher the ball will go). Keep watching the ball and follow through in the direction of your target so that your kicking leg finishes in a position horizontal to your waist.

DRILL 11
THE CIRCLE

Purpose: to practice accurate passing and ball control
Players: 5
Level: beginner to advanced
Equipment: 1 or 2 balls

This drill hones the skills of sidefoot passing (see Skill Box 1 on page 23), passing with the outside of the shoe (see Skill Box 13 on page 41), and trapping the ball (see Skill Boxes 3 and 4 on pages 25 and 26).

Players A, B, C, and D stand in a circle (diameter 25 yards/23 meters) around Player E, who stands in the middle. Player A passes the ball to Player E, who controls, turns, and passes the ball to Player B. B passes it back and E controls, turns, and passes to C. C then returns the ball to E and so on. When everyone has received the ball three times, player A goes into the middle of the circle and the process is repeated until each player has had a turn.

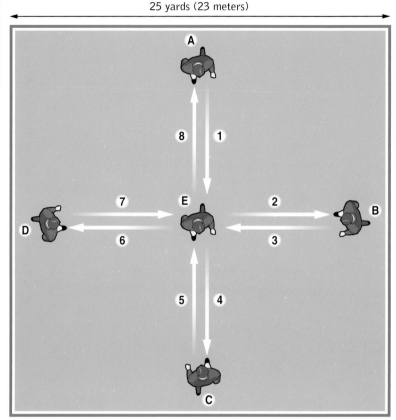

25 yards (23 meters)

COACH'S TIPS
- When Player E receives the ball, the coach or a designated player quickly shouts the name of one of the players in the circle and E has to pass the ball accurately to him.
- When Player E receives the ball the coach/player shouts the manner of pass he must play to which player (for example, "sidefoot to A"; "outside foot to B," and so on).
- The drill must be performed using each player's weaker foot only.
- Add another ball to the circle so that two are being passed around at once. This will make the drill much harder and faster, making players concentrate harder and forcing them to control and pass under pressure.

DRILL 12
THE TRIANGLE

10 yards (9 meters)

10 yards (9 meters)

Purpose: to practice control and passing with both feet
Players: 3
Level: beginner to advanced
Equipment: marker cones, ball

Players A and B stand on the baseline of a 10 x 10-yard (9 x 9-meter) grid, one at each end. Player C stands in the middle of the opposite baseline. Player A plays the ball up the line (straight in front of him up the side of the grid). Player C runs to collect the ball, controls it, and passes it diagonally to Player B with his right foot. Player B controls, and plays it up the right side of the grid.

Player C runs across, controls the ball, and with his left foot plays it diagonally back to A, who starts the process in motion again. The purpose of the drill is that Player C is having to control and play the ball with both feet. This is important because in match situations it is not always possible for a player to choose which foot he will control the ball with, and there may not be time to switch to his stronger foot. The basic skills are the same, but unless practiced it will feel less natural and more awkward to play the ball with the weaker foot.

After five sets, the players, following a minute's rest, swap positions.

◀ Eyal Berkovic, Israel's star midfielder, executes a perfect sidefoot pass.

DRILL 13
PIGGY IN THE MIDDLE

Purpose: to develop and practice control and passing under pressure, closing down, and intercepting
Players: 4 to 11
Level: beginner to advanced
Equipment: ball

Piggy in the middle (also called the controlled passing drill) is an excellent way to practice ball control, passing under pressure, and to generally fine-tune ball skills and improve alertness. It is a good exercise to do in the early stages of a training session as a preliminary drill after the players have properly warmed up and stretched.

Players A, B, C, and D stand in a circle around Player E. They pass among each other, calling for the ball, trying to stop E from getting a touch. E must try to close down on a player and intercept the ball, and when he touches it the last player to touch it before him has to go in the middle. As nobody wants to be the "piggy" they will try to ensure that their control is good and their passing as accurate as possible.

The game can be played with any number of participants — if numbers get larger the drill can be made more difficult by increasing the number of piggies.

DRILL 14
SHADOW PASSING

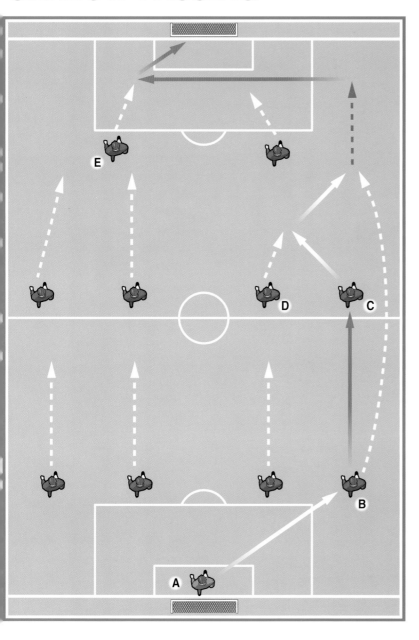

Purpose: to practice passing, lead passing, and receiving teamwork
Players: 11
Level: intermediate to advanced
Equipment: ball, full-size field

Shadow passing is trying to score a goal with no opposition. It is a good way for a team to practice their moves. The whole team should line up in their formation on the field. Typically you could employ a 4–4–2 formation, although the coach/players may change this depending on the way the team is to play.

In this example, the goalkeeper, Player A, rolls the ball out to the right defender, Player B, who passes it down the line to the right midfielder, Player C, and starts to make an overlapping run down the right wing. The right midfielder plays the ball across to the central midfielder, Player D, who plays it first time into the path of Player B. Player B controls the ball and delivers a cross pass to the far post, where the left-sided striker, Player E, has made a run and heads the ball into the goal.

During the move the rest of the players should make the moves and runs off the ball that they would make in a real match situation.

The coach or the players can practice different passing movements with different team formations in this way. You can also practice this drill in smaller groups – three or four players. When the team is used to the movement, opposition should be brought in to make it a more realistic exercise.

chapter three

USING YOUR HEAD

Soccer is known as "football" nearly worldwide for good reason. The foot is the most important part of the body in the game—but the head comes a close second. It is vital for every aspiring player to be able to head the ball in several different ways. (Remember the warning earlier, though; don't "fling" the head, but use it as an integral part of the whole body.)

A defender needs to be able to head the ball in order to clear any dangerous airborne balls coming his way, whether back up the field or into touch. The midfielder needs to be able to do the same, particularly from goal kicks that land around his territory. And the attacker, however tall or short, needs to be able to head the ball into the goal from crosses.

There are four major categories of header: the defensive header is aimed upward to try to gain as much distance on the ball as possible; the attacking header, one that is aimed at goal, should be directed down, so it is more difficult for the goalkeeper to save; the glancing header — which can be used for passing to a teammate or scoring — changes the direction of the ball slightly to fool a goalkeeper or take a defender out of the game; and the backheader, which sees the player direct the ball behind him so it maintains its original direction, is a highly useful tool at corners and throw-ins.

Most teams have heading specialists — usually their central defenders and strikers, but a midfielder who isn't skilled at heading is an incomplete midfielder. Even the goalkeeper has to occasionally head the ball. Remember that a team is unlikely to be able to win a game if they don't have players who can head the ball.

SOL CAMPBELL

England's Sol Campbell is a 6 foot 4 inch (190 centimeters) defender. With his height, immense strength, and perfect balance he is virtually unbeatable in the air. His strength and size give him a head start over most strikers, but it is concentration, timing, and bravery that are equally crucial in enabling him to be first to meet the ball and to deal with it effectively. He is also extremely dangerous in the opponent's box from corners and set pieces where he invariably goes forward and has scored many headed goals.

DRILL 15
HEADING WARM-UP

Purpose: to teach the basic body movements for heading, or to be used as part of pre-training or pre-match warm-up
Players: 1 to 30
Level: beginner to advanced
Equipment: none

Heading the ball is an action that requires the movement of the whole of your body, not just your head. This is a valuable exercise, then, to practice the body action needed to head the ball so you have an idea of what sort of muscles you are using. As part of a group or on your own, hold your arms out in front of you as if you were rowing a boat, then nod your head forward (jerking your elbows back and tensing your neck muscles at the same time) as if you were heading a ball.

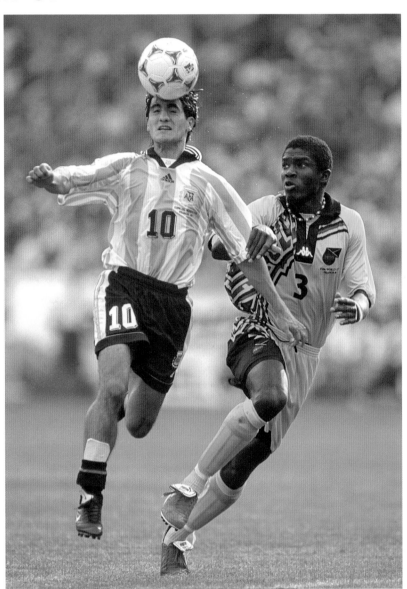

▲ Argentinian star, Ariel Ortega, gets to the ball first.

SKILL BOX   15

THROWING YOUR EYES AT THE BALL Some coaches describe the moment when you nod your head to make the header as "throwing your eyes at the ball." In other words, don't let the ball come to your head, but attack it positively. As the ball comes to you, keep watching it and at the last minute move your head forward (still watching the ball) to meet it.

DRILL 16
THE DEFENSIVE HEADER

SKILL BOX   16

JUMPING TO MEET A HEADER Jumping to head a soccer ball is all about timing. It is absolutely crucial to follow the path of the ball from the begining of its flight, adjusting your feet all the time so that you are in the correct position to meet the ball. You must concentrate on trying to head the ball at the highest point possible. If you can, take a starting run and launch yourself into the air by springing off your stronger foot, bringing your arms up and putting your elbows out for balance (be careful, no fouls!). If you have timed your jump correctly you will be in a position to meet the ball with your head while you are still in the air. But, if you take your eyes off the ball for even a split second, the chances are that you'll miss it altogether.

Purpose: to practice heading technique and instill confidence
Players: 2
Level: beginner to advanced
Equipment: ball

Player A stands 6 yards (5 meters) from Player B and throws the ball underarm to him at head height (so he doesn't have to jump). Player B waits for the ball and, when it makes contact with his forehead, heads it firmly back to Player A. After 10 successful headers in a row, the players swap roles.

Drill 16
PROGRESSION
Purpose: to practice jumping to head the ball
Players: 2
Level: beginner to advanced
Equipment: ball

Jumping to head the ball is the next stage. Players A and B should stand 8 yards (7 meters) apart. Player A throws the ball (underarm) slightly higher in the air than the basic drill. The throw should be such that Player B has to jump to meet the ball in the air (see Skill Box 16) and head it back to Player A. Players should be encouraged to meet the ball and head it at the highest point possible. This gives the best chance in a match situation of beating an opponent to the ball. You should get power (and so height and distance) and direction on headers, the idea being to clear the ball from danger. Challenge Player B to head the ball back over the head of Player A.

USING YOUR HEAD 51

DRILL 17
HEADING TRIANGLE

Purpose: to practice heading timing and technique
Players: 3
Level: beginner to advanced
Equipment: marker cones, 2 balls

Set up a 10 x 10-yard (9 x 9-meter) grid. Player A stands in the center of the grid, with players B and C standing at either corner of the baseline. Player B throws a ball underarm into the air at Player A, who heads it back to him. Then Player C throws a ball to Player A. This means that Player A has to turn and head it back. Players B and C should vary the height and pace of the throws so that occasionally Player A will have to jump or stoop. B and C can also quicken the rate of the throws after a while, making the drill more challenging.

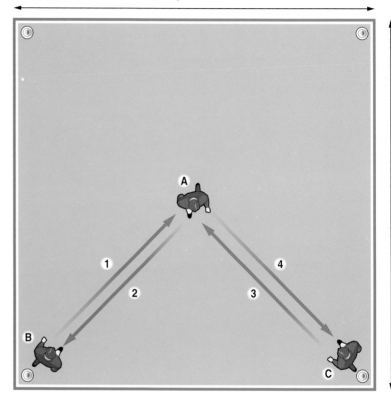

10 yards (9 meters)

10 yards (9 meters)

Argentina's Nelson Vivas rises high to head clear. ▶

SKILL BOX   17

HEADING A LONG, HIGH BALL As with all heading, when dealing with a long, high ball, it is essential to follow its flight all the way and not take your eyes off it even for a split second. It takes great concentration to follow the ball and move your feet into position so that you are right under it, balanced and steady, as it comes to you. Remember to shout your name to your teammates to let them know you are going for the ball, otherwise you will all bump into each other. If someone else shouts before you, even if you think you are in a better position, you must get out of their way. Once you are in position then you must jump to meet the ball at the highest point possible — if you have a free header you can keep your feet on the ground and head it cleanly and firmly. The crucial thing is to get into the right position and have the confidence to meet the ball firmly, sending it right back along its flight path (into the air where it will travel some distance back the other way). When you get more confident, you can head the ball above its original flight path, therefore nodding it directly into the path of one of your teammates.

DRILL 18
HEADING THE HIGH BALL

Purpose: to practice timing and technique for defensive heading of long balls
Players: 3
Level: beginners to advanced
Equipment: ball, full-size field

One use of the defensive header is to head the ball back in the direction it came from after an opponent has kicked it into his own half. Player A, a goalkeeper, kicks the ball toward Players B and C, who stand on the edge of the center circle in the half of the field opposite to Player A. Players B and C must head the ball back, not letting it bounce. This is also a good drill to practice defensive communication, because the two defenders must talk to each other to decide which one of them is going to go for the header. The player who believes he is in the better position to make the header must call his own name, loud enough and early enough for the other player to keep out of his way.

Drill 18
PROGRESSION
Purpose: to practice defensive headers under pressure
Players: 5
Level: intermediate to advanced
Equipment: ball, full-size field

Once Players B and C are comfortably heading the ball back, add Player D and later Player E as opposing strikers. These players must challenge for the ball too. Remind the players that caution should be exercised so that nobody gets injured.

DRILL 19
HEADING AWAY A CROSS

Purpose: to practice effective clearance headers from crosses
Players: 3
Level: beginner to advanced
Equipment: ball, full-size field

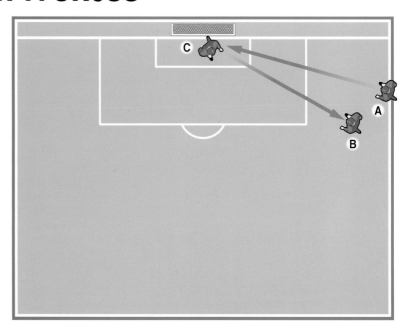

When you're heading a cross, the ball needs to be headed away at an angle, clearing it to the safest part of the field — out wide but as far up the field as possible.

To practice this, Player A puts a long throw into the penalty area while Player B stands 2 yards (2 meters) outside the box, even with the corner of it (on the same side as Player A). From a starting point anywhere in the six-yard box Player C must head the ball to Player B. It is important to get power and accuracy in this header, taking the ball from a position of danger to a position of relative safety.

**Drill 19
PROGRESSION
Purpose:** to practice effective clearance headers from crosses
Players: 4
Level: intermediate to advanced
Equipment: bibs, ball

Add Player D, an opposing striker, to the drill. Player D will attempt to challenge for the ball, making Player C's job of clearing it much harder. More defending and attacking players can be added to the drill and the ball can be delivered as a cross rather than throw.

SKILL BOX 18

ANGLED DEFENSIVE HEADING
In this movement you are heading the ball away at an angle of about 45–60 degrees. Approach the ball in the same way, but make contact with the side of your forehead (the side corresponding with the direction you want the ball to travel in) and as you make contact nod your head and twist your body the way you want the ball to go. Remember that power is crucial because you must clear the ball as far as possible, so attack it and use all the strength in your neck as you make the header.

Giant Dutch defender Jaap Stam ▶ wins the ball and heads it to safety.

DRILL 20
RUNNING AND HEADING

10 yards (9 meters)

10 yards (9 meters)

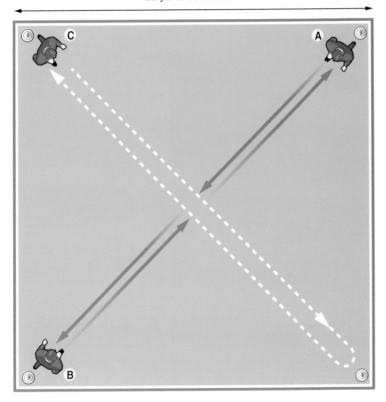

Purpose: to practice heading while running
Players: 3
Level: beginner to advanced
Equipment: marker cones, 2 balls

Set up a 10 x 10-yard (9 x 9-meter) grid. Two players (A and B), who will deliver the balls, stand at opposite corners of the grid. Player C stands in a third corner. Player C runs into the center of the grid, and as he begins his run Player A throws the ball underarm into the air in front of him. Player C heads the ball firmly back to Player A and continues running to the far corner. When he reaches the corner he turns around and runs back into the center as Player B throws a ball into the air, underarm, for him to head. Player C heads it back to B, continues running to the corner where he started, and then the whole process is repeated. After 10 headers the players swap positions.

SKILL BOX   19

THE ATTACKING HEADER
To direct the ball downward you must head nearer the top of the ball — and nod your head and twist your body downward in the direction you want it to go. To get power you must really attack the ball, using your neck muscles and the movement of your upper body to meet it with some force and punch it in the direction of the target.

HEADING FOR GOAL

Purpose: to practice the skill of powerfully heading downward for goal

Players: 3

Level: intermediate to advanced

Equipment: half a full-size field, bibs (to identify attacking and defensive players), 10 balls

Exactly what kind of header is required for an attempt on goal depends very much on the individual situation: where the goalkeeper is standing, how many defenders are between the attacking player and the goal, the speed of the pass, and so on. However, a powerful downward header is often, though not always, the most effective way of beating the goalkeeper. This is because the ball lands low, away from the keeper's hands, and also means that there may be an awkward bounce for him to deal with.

To practice this, Player A stands on the sideline, even with the corner of the penalty area. Player B stands on the edge of the "D" at the edge of the penalty area with a ball. Player B passes the ball wide, in front of Player A, who runs onto it, takes a touch, and plays a cross into the penalty area. Player B, in the meantime, runs into the area to meet the ball with a firm, downward header (see Skill Box 19 on page 55) aimed at the bottom corner of the goal. Player C, a goalkeeper, must try to save the header. Player A should vary the speed and direction of his crosses so that Player B can practice heading in a variety of situations.

▲ Powerful English striker, Dion Dublin, scores one of his many headed goals.

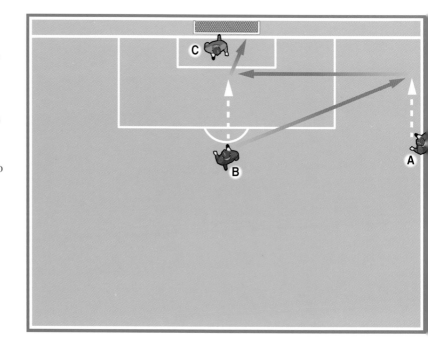

DRILL 22
TIMING THE RUN

Purpose: to practice the skills of timing an attacking run into the box, defending a cross, and crossing the ball
Players: 4
Level: intermediate to advanced
Equipment: half a full-size field, bibs (to identify attacking and defensive players), ball

In this drill two attacking players, A and B, play against one defender, Player C, plus a goalkeeper, Player D. Start with the ball on the edge of the box with Player A. He plays it wide to Player B. Player B must fire in a cross (from somewhere outside the penalty area), with Player A timing his run to try to beat Player C to the ball and head it into the goal.

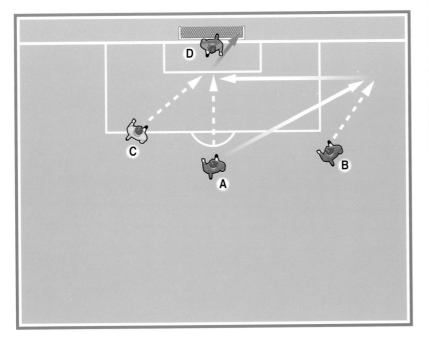

Drill 22
PROGRESSION
Purpose: to practice the skills of timing an attacking run into the box, defending a cross, and crossing the ball under pressure
Players: 5
Level: intermediate to advanced
Equipment: half a full-size field, bibs (to identify attacking and defensive players), ball

Make it a two-against-two game with Player A having to time his run to beat two defenders instead of one. This demands extremely intelligent running off the ball and is also good defensive practice for the defenders, and crossing practice for Player B.

DRILL 23
THE GLANCING HEADER

Purpose: to practice the technique of the glancing header
Players: 3
Level: intermediate to advanced
Equipment: marker cones, 5 balls

Players A and B stand opposite each other along the baseline of a 10 x 10-yard (9 x 9-meter) grid. Player C stands in the center of the grid, 5 yards (5 meters) from the baseline. Player A throws the ball (throw-in style) to player C, who takes a short run-up performs a glancing header to Player B. Player B then throws the ball in and Player C glances it to Player A and so on. Players A and B alter the height, speed, and frequency of their throws. After five minutes the players swap roles.

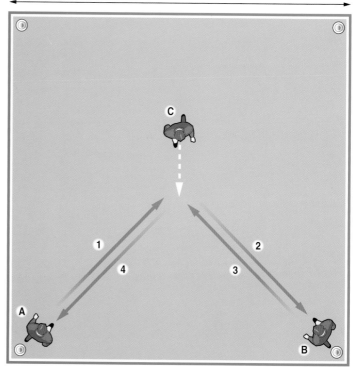

10 yards (9 meters)

10 yards (9 meters)

SKILL BOX 20

THE GLANCING HEADER

A glancing header is performed by glancing the head in the direction of the ball as contact is made. Contact is light rather than firm, meaning that the ball should slightly, rather than drastically, change direction. This header can be used to score a goal, guiding the ball into the corner of the net, but also to ease the ball to a teammate or assist a dangerous cross into the box.

▶ Dwight Yorke of Trinidad and Tobago glances the ball into the net for Manchester United.

58   **USING YOUR HEAD**

DRILL 24
THE DIVING HEADER

20 yards (18 meters)

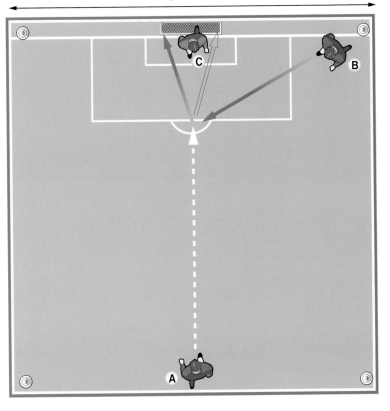

20 yards (18 meters)

Purpose: to practice the skill of the diving header
Players: 3
Level: intermediate to advanced
Equipment: marker cones, full-size goal, 10 balls

There are few more satisfying ways to score a goal than with a diving header. They require bravery, timing, and technique. A diving header may also be used to clear the ball in defensive situations or even to win possession in midfield.

To do this drill safely it should be practiced on a soft surface or in a gym using mats.

Set up a 20 x 20-yard (18 x 18-meter) grid with a goal on one side. Player A stands on the side of the grid opposite the goal. Player B stands in the corner of the grid next to the goal, and Player C, a goalkeeper, should be in position. Player A makes a run, Player B crosses the ball — aiming ahead of the receiver, 3 or 4 feet (1 meter) off the ground —and Player A dives at it, attempting to head it into the goal.

SKILL BOX   21

THE DIVING HEADER When attempting a diving header you must concentrate extremely hard on the flight of the ball. When you are sure that you can reach it by diving forward, time your run against the flight of the ball and then launch yourself into what can only be described as a dive at the ball. Bring your arms forward and away from your body for balance, and simply concentrate on making a firm connection. Your dive will automatically give the header power (if you make a good connection, especially if the cross is coming at you hard). If you want the ball to go straight (the way you are pointing) then you won't need to direct it; just make sure you meet the ball toward the middle. If you get underneath it, it will fly into the air. If you need to direct it then try to use your neck and shoulder muscles as you would with other types of header.

DRILL 25
THE BACKHEADER

Purpose: to develop and practice the skill of backheading
Players: 3
Level: beginner to advanced
Equipment: marker cones, 5 balls

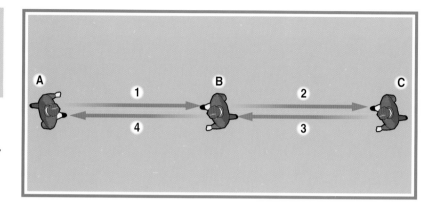

From a marked-out distance of 8 yards (7 meters), Player A throws the ball (throw-in style) to Player B, who backheads the ball (see Skill Box 22 on page 61) to Player C, who is standing 8 yards (7 meters) behind him. Player B turns around and Player C then throws the ball, reversing the process. The serving players, A and C, should vary the height and speed of the balls they throw, ensuring that on occasions they force Player B to jump and backhead the ball so that he practices a range of movements.

Drill 25
PROGRESSION
Purpose: to test and develop the skill of backheading under pressure
Players: 4
Level: intermediate to advanced
Equipment: marker cones, 5 balls

Add a defender, Player D, to the drill. He must stand behind Player B (whichever way he is facing). He should challenge for the ball, although, if the delivery of the throw is good, he should find it very difficult to steal the ball without pushing or fouling

Player B, who will be first to the ball because of his position. This is why the backheader is very difficult to defend at free kicks and corners and why opposing teams often place two defenders on an attacker looking to get in a backheader (one player in front of him and one behind).

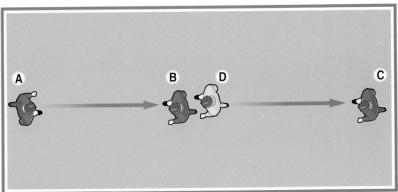

◀ Paolo Wanchope of Costa Rica creates havoc in the box with this perfect backheader.

SKILL BOX 22

THE BACKHEADER Performed by deflecting the ball with the back of the head so that it continues in almost the direction it is going, but with a slightly altered path. It is useful as an attacking weapon to create confusion and as a defensive move to head back to the keeper. Because the ball is usually going at some speed, this slight alteration of speed and trajectory can create confusion in the opponents' penalty area or, in open play, extend the distance of a throw-in or ball kicked upfield.

It is quite a difficult skill to perfect since you need to make only slight contact with the ball. As the ball comes toward you, time your jump so that you flick your head and upper body back (mimicking the flight of the ball), letting the ball deflect off your forehead as it goes over the top of you. The faster the ball is going, the less contact needed.

chapter four

SHARP SHOOTING

No matter how hard a team works, if they can't shoot straight, that work will go to waste. Shooting produces about three-quarters of all goals, and the more practiced a team is, the better they will become at scoring.

Shooting can be performed from all distances using a variety of techniques. Power shooting from outside the box — even from your own territory — is done using the instep and a big follow-through. This can produce some of the most spectacular goals. However, a simple sidefoot pass into the net can be just as effective for scoring a goal and no less valuable to the result. A shot can be volleyed — when the ball is in the air, half-volleyed — when it is on the bounce, curled with the inside or outside of the foot, and, perhaps best of all, chipped over the despairing goalkeeper.

There is a choice when you are about to take a shot, between power and accuracy. If a shot is powerful and on target, it has a good chance of beating the goalkeeper. But if a shot is accurate it doesn't need much power to get past the keeper. It is important to practice both types of shot in order to have variety in your play.

Another important aspect of shooting is the ability to take good penalties (again, choosing between accuracy and power), particularly in the modern game when so many matches are decided, after extra time, on penalties, and when referees are more likely to point to the spot because of law changes favoring attackers.

ANDREI SHEVCHENKO

Ukrainian striker Andrei Shevchenko is one of the fastest players in the world — and also one of the most feared sharpshooters. Shevchenko is a master at finding the unguarded hole between the goalkeeper and his post, but he can also blast the ball so hard that few keepers stand a chance of stopping the ball. Like all masters of their craft, Shevchenko has spent hours on the training field perfecting his shooting.

DRILL 26
TARGET PRACTICE

Purpose: to practice accurate shooting for goal
Players: 1 to 5
Level: beginner to advanced
Equipment: wall, chalk, 10 balls

Here's a simple way to practice shooting. Mark four targets on a wall. Mark up a full-size goal (posts 8 feet/2 meters) high, crossbar 8 yards/7 meters long), then mark four circles each 2 feet (60 centimeters) in diameter, one in each bottom corner and one in each top corner. These are the optimum places to aim for when shooting, the parts of the goal that are most difficult for the goalkeeper, placed in the center of the goal, to reach. Practice shooting at these targets from distances ranging from 10 yards (9 meters) to 30 yards (27 meters) —with the inside and outside of your feet as well as with the instep and the sidefoot. You should practice shooting with both feet because chances will come to you when you need to strike the ball with your weaker foot. Even professional players miss goals because they attempt a shot with their stronger foot when their weaker one is better positioned.

SKILL BOX 23

SHOOTING There are many different ways of shooting for goal, incorporating skills that have already been worked on. For example, you can sidefoot the ball into the net, strike the ball with your instep, volley it, or drive it. All of these skills will be looked at in detail, but remember that when you are shooting you must always keep your head down over the ball as you strike it. This will keep the ball down, whereas if you lean back, the ball is likely to fly into the air over the crossbar. The most important thing of all is to get your shot on target. Even if the goalkeeper saves it, you may win a corner or the ball may rebound to a teammate (or you) to provide another scoring opportunity.

COACH'S TIPS
- The coach or another player shouts "left" or "right" as Player B controls the ball and he must shoot into the appropriate corner.
- Player B has to one time the ball instead of controlling it first.
- A goalkeeper stands on his line and runs out to block the goal as soon as the server passes the ball. Player B has to shoot the ball past him.
- All these drills are practiced with Player B's weaker foot.

HITTING THE MARK

Purpose: to practice accurate sidefoot shooting
Players: 2 to 20
Level: intermediate to advanced
Equipment: 10 balls, 2 marker cones, half of a full-size field, full-size goal

You often see the top professional strikers picking their spot and sidefooting the ball into the net when they see a space left by the goalkeeper, almost as if they were passing the ball into the goal. The sidefoot strike is accurate and, if the technique is good, it can still be hit with a degree of power.

Place a cone along the goalline 1 yard (1 meter) in from each post of a full-size goal. Player A stands in the center of the field, 8 yards (7 meters) outside the penalty area. Player B stands on the edge of the "D" on the edge of the penalty area. Player A passes the ball along the ground toward the penalty spot. Player B runs into the penalty area, controls the ball with one touch, and then sidefoots — aiming for the gap between one of the cones and the post. A whole squad of players can be involved in this drill, lining up behind Player B. After Player B has had his shot, he runs to fetch the ball (which is hopefully in the net) and Player A plays another ball to the next player in line.

For further variations see Coach's Tips on page 64.

DRILL 28
FAR-POST FINISHING

Purpose: to practice first-time close-range shooting
Players: 2 to 20
Level: beginner to advanced
Equipment: half a full-size field, full-size goal, 10 balls

When a professional gets a "tap-in" at the far post he makes it look easy. It isn't. He has practiced the skill over and over again on the training field.

Player A stands anywhere outside the penalty area and passes the ball to a wide man, Player B, who is standing 2 yards (2 meters) in from the goalline on the edge of the box. Player B controls the ball and then crosses it low and hard, across the goal to the edge of the six-yard box, to the far post. Player A has made a run to this spot and he sidefoots the ball first time (if the ball is not coming too fast he may elect to drive it rather than sidefoot it, although sidefooting gives a greater chance of accuracy) into the corner of the net. This routine can involve a large group of players, with other members of the squad lining up behind Player B and completing the same drill after the player in front has had his turn.

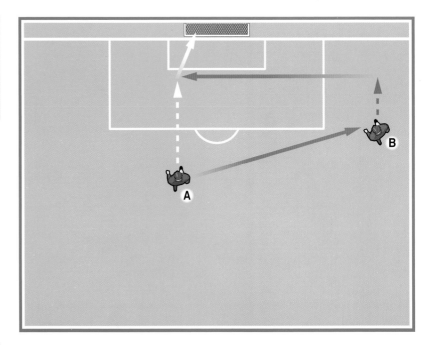

SKILL BOX   24

SIDEFOOT SHOOTING The skills
used in sidefoot shooting are
essentially identical to those practiced
in sidefoot passing (see Skill Box 1 on
page 23). The only real difference is
that you can use as much power as you
can generate because you don't have
to worry about a receiving teammate
having to control it. Also, you may be
in a situation where you can disguise
the direction of your shot by
positioning to shoot in one direction,
then at the last moment altering your
body, leg, and foot positions and
sidefooting the ball the other way.
Initially, however, just concentrate on
making good contact with the ball and
hitting the target.

◀ Poaching at the far post can win matches
as Solskjaer (Manchester United) proved
in the Champions League.

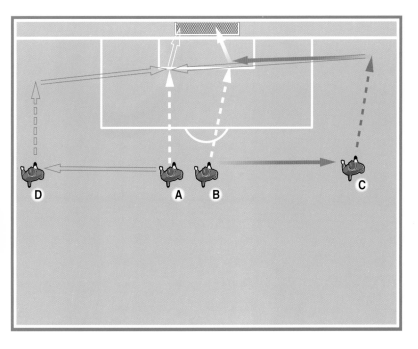

Drill 28
PROGRESSION
Purpose: to practice running off
the ball and getting into goal-
scoring positions
Players: 4
Level: intermediate to advanced
Equipment: half a full-size field

Repeat the drill with two attackers
(A and B) and two wingers (C and
D). A and B start in the center of
the field, 20 yards (18 meters) from
goal. B passes to C, who is standing
20 yards (18 meters) to his right.
C makes a run to the goalline while
A and B make far- and near-post
runs. C crosses in, to either the
near or far post, where the
appropriate striker sidefoots the
ball into the goal. Then the process
is repeated using the left winger
(D). For variation, make A and B
cross over occasionally, so A runs to
the near post and B to the far.

DRILL 29
LEFT- OR RIGHT-FOOT DRILL

Purpose: to develop the skill of adjusting the body quickly to make a shot
Players: 2 to 20
Level: intermediate to advanced
Equipment: half a full-size field, full-size goal, 10 balls

Players need to be able to adjust their body and feet quickly to get in shots on goal. Rarely will a player have enough time to do more than make an instantaneous decision to shoot, reacting instinctively to where the ball is and where he wants it to go.

In this drill, Player A, the server, stands just outside the "D" at the edge of the penalty area. The players stand in the center of the field, 10 yards (9 meters) behind him toward the center circle. Player B passes the ball along the ground to Player A and starts his run toward goal to accept the return. Player A controls it and lays it off to either the left or the right, so that it runs to the edge of the box. Player B must alter his run according to which side the ball has gone and shoots the ball at goal with his appropriate foot. After he has had his shot he must retrieve the ball, then the next player in line assumes the role of Player B.

COACH'S TIPS
- Add a goalkeeper to make the drill more realistic.
- A defender, Player C, runs out from the six-yard box when the server releases the ball and attempts to block the shot.

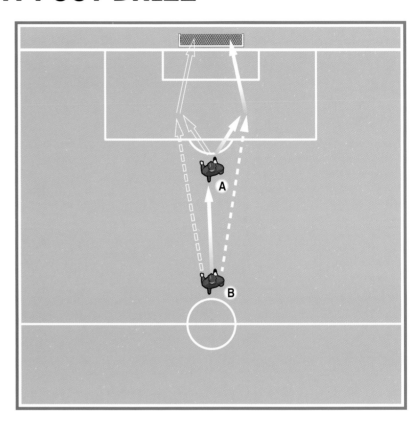

▼ When Croatian Davor Suker gets a chance, he usually hits the target.

DRILL 30
VOLLEYING

Purpose: to practice basic volleying skills
Players: 2
Level: beginner
Equipment: ball

Drill 30
PROGRESSION A
Purpose: to practice volleying shooting skills
Players: 2 to 10
Level: beginner to intermediate
Equipment: 10 balls, full-size goal

Drill 30
PROGRESSION B
Purpose: to practice volleying toward goal from a cross
Players: 2
Level: intermediate to advanced
Equipment: 10 balls, full-size goal

One of the most spectacular ways to score a goal is on the volley. The play requires superb timing as the ball is hit in the air with power. If a volley is on target, the goalkeeper stands very little chance of saving it unless he just happens to be in the right place. Volleying requires more practice to perfect than almost any other skill in soccer (see Skill Box 6 on page 28).

Player A stands 5 yards (4.5 meters) from Player B and throws the ball to him underarm, aiming for it to reach him 3 feet (1 meter) off the ground (this height should be lowered for younger or shorter players). Player B volleys the ball back to him with his stronger foot. Then the players should repeat the exercise, this time with Player B using his weaker foot. Practice the half-volley if the ball lands at your feet.

Player A stands on the penalty spot facing Player B, who stands 5 yards (5 meters) to one side of A. Player B throws the ball underarm, about 3 feet (1 meter) in the air, so it falls between Player A and the goal. Player A must turn, following the flight of the ball, and volley it into the goal. Use a goalkeeper to make the drill more difficult and realistic. Players can line up behind Player B, taking turns to volley. Once a player has had a shot, he must retrieve the ball and then return to the back of the line and wait for his next turn.

Player A stands inside the "D" at the edge of the penalty area and passes the ball to Player B, who is standing on the edge of the penalty area. Player B controls the ball and plays a cross, aiming it between the penalty spot and the six-yard line, 2 or 3 feet (1 meter) off the ground. Player A, meanwhile, has run into the box anticipating the cross, and volleys toward goal.

A goalkeeper and defenders can be added to make the drill more realistic and challenging.

SKILL BOX   25

HIP-SWING VOLLEY This is used when you have to connect with the ball a little higher (up to 1 yard/1 meter off the ground). Again, put your weight on the ball of your nonkicking foot, but this time angle your foot toward the ball (e.g., if the ball is coming from the right, point your toes to the right). Turn your body so that your left shoulder (if you are right-footed) is in line with your foot. Watch the ball and as it approaches swing your foot in the air, twisting your shoulder and hips to the left and swiveling on the ball of your foot. This will allow your kicking foot to reach higher off the ground. Connect with the ball with your instep—the laced part of your shoe.

DRILL 31
POWER SHOOTING

Purpose: to practice power-shooting techniques
Players: 2 to 20
Level: beginner to advanced
Equipment: full-size goal, 10 balls

Player A, the server, stands on the line of the "D" at the edge of the penalty area. Player B stands 5 yards (5 meters) in front of him, away from the goal. Player B plays the ball to Player A, and begins to move toward the goal. Player A plays the ball into Player B's path and he shoots for goal first time, trying to hit the ball low and hard into the bottom corner. The ball should be hit with the instep, and the players should keep their heads down and their bodies over the ball as they make contact.

Drill 31
PROGRESSION
Purpose: to practice long-range shooting
Players: 6
Level: intermediate to advanced
Equipment: marker cones, full-size goal, 10 balls

Lay out markers 20, 25, 30, 35, and 40 yards (18, 23, 27, 32, and 36.5 meters) from the goal in the center area of the field. Player A passes the ball 20 yards (18 meters) out to Player B, who tries to power-shoot the ball past the goalkeeper. If he succeeds, he moves further out to 25 yards (23 meters) on his next turn after all four players have shot. If he misses he stays on 20 yards (18 meters). To add a competitive element to the drill, the winner is the player who has scored from furthest out.

COACH'S TIP

Power shooting is a good drill for the end of a practice session. Line up all the players, and have them shoot one by one (as in the basic drill, with one player passing the ball off on the edge of the box) from just outside the box.

DRILL 32
CHIPPING

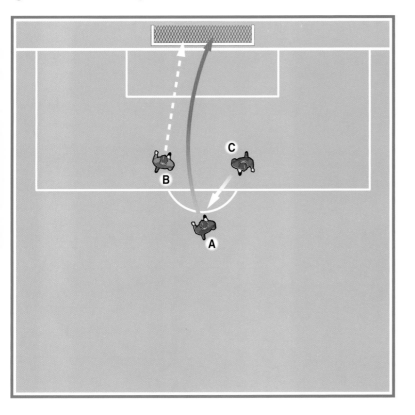

Purpose: to practice chipping techniques
Players: 3
Level: beginner to advanced
Equipment: marker cones, 3 balls

Undoubtedly, the most graceful way to score a goal is to chip the goalkeeper (see Skill Box 26). The sight of the ball arcing in the air over the keeper and dropping under the crossbar is magnificent — all the more so since it's a very difficult skill to achieve and is executed very rarely, even in professional games.

The simplest way to practice chipping is for two players to chip the ball to one another, varying the distance between them. But here are a couple of games to make the drill more interesting.

Lay out a 20 x 10-yard (18 x 9-meter) grid. Players A and B stand on each baseline; Player C stands in the middle. Keeping the ball in the grid, Players A and B have to chip it over player C to each other. If Player C — who is not allowed to move forward or backward — manages to touch the ball, the players swap positions.

Drill 32
PROGRESSION
Purpose: to practice chipping technique
Players: 3
Level: intermediate to advanced
Equipment: full-size goal, 5 balls

Player A stands 25 yards (23 meters) from the goal in the center of the field. Player B, a goalkeeper, stands with Player C, the server, on the edge of the box. Player C gently passes the ball to Player A, at which point Player B, the goalkeeper, starts running back to his line. Player A has to chip the ball into the net before Player B can return to guard it.

SKILL BOX   26

THE CHOP CHIP Place your nonkicking foot next to the ball as if you were about to sidefoot or drive it, but stand slightly further forward so that you are almost standing over the ball. Push your kicking foot downward in a short, sharp movement into the space between the ball and the ground, catching the edge of the ball on the way to create backspin. The ball should "chip" into the air. The spin will make it harder for the goalkeeper to make a save.

DRILL 33
PENALTIES

Purpose: to practice penalty-taking techniques
Players: 6 to 8
Level: beginner to advanced
Equipment: full-size goal, 5 balls

Every member of the team — not just the team's designated penalty taker — should be able to score from the penalty spot, so practicing penalties should be a frequent part of any training program. If nothing else, it's good training for shooting accuracy, and good practice for goalkeepers.

Set up a sudden-death competition, using six to eight players. When a player misses a penalty (or the goalkeeper saves it), that player is out of the competition, and has to jog around the field as a forfeit. The winner is the last player left in the competition. If he is regularly the winner of the competitions, he should become the team's penalty shooter in matches.

SKILL BOX 27

PENALTY-TAKING Scoring a penalty in a match situation is as much about confidence, nerve, and concentration as it is about technique. However, there are several ways to strike a ball. Some players drive it at the target as powerfully as they can, relying on its speed to beat the keeper. Others sidefoot or curve the ball with the inside of their foot into the corners, knowing that if they are accurate the keeper can't reach the ball, even if he dives the right way. Another option, if you can see that the goalkeeper is about to dive to one side or the other, is to blast the ball straight toward the center of the goal.

DRILL 34
PENALTY ACCURACY DRILL

Purpose: to teach and practice more accurate penalty taking
Players: 6 to 8
Level: intermediate to advanced
Equipment: full-size goal, 2 marker cones, 5 balls

Place a cone 2 feet (1 meter) away from each post. Six to eight players line up and practice hitting penalties into the spaces between the cone and the post. Once the players are getting it right nearly every time, on both sides, remove the cones, put a goalkeeper in place, and the players should aim for the same spot. They should score just about every time.

◀ Ex-England international Keith Curle makes no mistake.

chapter five

RUNNING WITH THE BALL

There's nothing more exciting than the sight of a player running at the defense with the ball, ready to take out a defender by dribbling past him, then delivering a cross or a shot.

While dribbling is less evident in the modern game than it was in earlier days (teams have realized that passing movements stand more chance of success), it is still a highly important part of every player's repertoire —including the goalkeeper's. It must be stressed that dribbling shouldn't be overused. There's nothing as frustrating as a player who always runs with the ball and never passes, but when used in moderation, it can be a brilliant tactic that can unlock the tightest of defenses.

Dribbling is the ability to run with the ball at your feet, sometimes looking at it, sometimes not, and to trick your way past an opponent. Various tricks can be used: the classic dummy where the player feints to go one way and then goes another; the nutmeg, where he puts the ball through the opponent's legs and runs around; the footover, whereby the player rolls his foot over the ball before moving it in a new direction; or the simple pass and sprint, where outrunning your opponent is the key.

Some players dribble almost exclusively with one foot, but the best ones are able to use both. Only a good deal of practice makes you adept at dribbling and able to get

JUNINHO

What Brazilian midfield star Juninho lacks in size and strength he more than makes up for with his dribbling ability. By being able to keep the ball under control at his feet while running at speed, constantly changing speed and direction, feinting and dummying defenders with subtle movements of his legs and upper body, he is able to make breathtaking surges up the field. Sometimes this skill enables him to beat three or four opposing players at one time, taking them out of the game in a split-second and suddenly creating an attacking opportunity from nowhere.

DRILL 35
JOGGING WITH THE BALL

Purpose: to develop and practice dribbling techniques
Players: 1
Level: beginner to intermediate
Equipment: ball

It is essential that you become confident while running with the ball at your feet. The best way to do this is to practice dribbling. You can do this during a team practice or on your own time.

You should simply run with the ball at your feet, practicing using both the inside and the outside of the foot to keep the ball under control. At first you should keep your eye on the ball, but when you become more confident you should practice occasionally glancing up, looking for possible passing or shooting options.

You should also practice changing speed, occasionally bursting into a sprint, and changing direction by pushing the ball with the outside of the foot in the direction you are moving — in other words, use the outside of the left foot when moving left and vice versa, and then follow in the direction of the ball. The more you practice, the more confident you will become on the move with the ball.

DRILL 36
THE CONE DRILL

Purpose: to develop and practice dribbling skills
Players: 1 to 10
Level: beginner to advanced
Equipment: marker cones, ball

This is a drill used by professional soccer teams to improve players' dribbling ability.

Place seven cones in a line, 5 feet (2 meters) from one another. Player A must dribble the ball through the cones, turn around, and dribble back through them again, mainly swapping from the inside of his kicking foot to the outside of the same foot to change direction. When he has finished, the next player sets off.

Drill 36
PROGRESSION A
Purpose: to improve dribbling
Players: 1 to 10
Level: intermediate to advanced
Equipment: marker cones, ball, stopwatch

Each player is timed with a stopwatch, encouraging him to try to improve his time with each run.

Drill 36
PROGRESSION B
Purpose: to perfect and sharpen dribbling skills
Players: 1 to 10
Level: intermediate to advanced
Equipment: marker cones, ball

Reduce the distance between the cones to 4 and then 3 feet (1.5 meters and 90 centimeters), to make the drill more challenging.

Drill 36
PROGRESSION C
Purpose: to encourage speed and accuracy when dribbling
Players: 2 to 20
Level: intermediate to advanced
Equipment: marker cones, ball

Set up two or three parallel lines of cones (vary the distance between cones depending on the ability of the participating players). The players race one on one as they dribble. Remember, precision must be allied with speed; if the ball hits more than one cone the player must return to the beginning and start again. This drill can be done as a relay race, involving two or more teams and every player in the squad.

Drill 36
PROGRESSION D
Purpose: to practice dribbling at speed in a match situation
Players: 1 to 10
Level: intermediate to advanced
Equipment: marker cones, 10 balls, full-size goal

Set up a line of cones that ends 25 yards (23 meters) from the goal. After completing a run each dribbler shoots for goal. The drill can be carried out with or without a goalkeeper. This makes the exercise more realistic, tests players' ability to shoot after a long, strenuous run, and also, importantly, makes the drill enjoyable for those taking part.

DRILL 37
SPEED DRIBBLING

Purpose: to practice the skill of running with the ball at speed
Players: 4
Level: beginner to advanced
Equipment: half a full-size field, marker cones, 4 balls

Line up four players on the goalline, place a cone or other marker opposite each person on the halfway line. The players must dribble up the field, around the cone, and return as fast as they can. The first one to cross back over the goalline at the point he started from is the winner.

USA star Mia Hamm builds up speed. ▶

Drill 37
PROGRESSION A
Purpose: to work on the basic skill of speed dribbling
Players: 2 to 11
Level: beginner to advanced
Equipment: marker cones, 4 balls, half a full-size field, full-size goal

This exercise is essentially the same as the basic drill except the players set off one by one, dribble past the cone, turn around, dribble back, and shoot the ball into the goal, which is guarded by a goalkeeper.

Drill 37
PROGRESSION B
Purpose: to perfect the skill of speed dribbling
Players: 3 to 11
Level: advanced
Equipment: marker cones, 4 balls, half a full-size field, full-size goal

Add a defender who must be dribbled around before the player shoots for goal on the way back from the cone. Keep a note of each player's score to add an element of competition.

Here are some tricks the dribbler can use to get past the defender.

PASS AND SPRINT This move is best performed at speed. When you are confronted by a defender you play the ball to the right of him, run around him, and pick up the ball again behind him.

THE DUMMY When confronted by a defender you put your weight on your left foot and feint to push the ball to his right with the inside of your right foot. It is important that you put your weight on the ball of your foot to give you more mobility. If you can see that the defender is responding to your dummy, push the ball with the outside of the right foot to his left instead, and run after the ball into the space you have created.

THE FOOTOVER This play is best done at slower speeds. You are confronted by a defender in front of you. You feint to play the ball to your left by moving the instep of your right foot toward the ball and your weight onto your left foot. Instead of hitting the ball to the right, pass your foot over the ball, and then push it to the right into space, past the defender with the outside of your right foot. If the defender "buys" the dummy he will be left wrong-footed and you will be able to run past him in the other direction.

THE CRUYFF TURN This skill was made famous by the Dutch midfielder Johan Cruyff, whom most coaches considered to be the best player in the world in the mid-1970s. Feint to shoot or cross with the inside of your right foot, putting your weight onto your left. Instead of following through, drag the ball with your toe behind your left foot, and move your weight onto your right foot. This skill is still most widely used by Dutch players—Dennis Bergkamp for example.

THE NUTMEG This trick can be used if a defender is standing squarely in front of you. Push the ball between his legs and run around him to pick up the ball.

▲ Italy's Roberto Baggio has plenty of tricks up his sleeve.

▲ Mark Keller of England's West Ham, on the move.

▲ Ronaldo of Brazil weighs up his options.

▲ Paul Telfer of England's Coventry City shows off his skills.

DRILL 38
"SHOW US A TRICK"

Purpose: to develop and practice dribbling improvisation
Players: 2 to 10
Level: intermediate to advanced
Equipment: ball

Player A passes the ball to Player B, who is standing 15 yards (14 meters) in front of him. Player B controls the ball and runs toward Player A, who shouts "show us a trick" when Player B is in front of him. Player B performs the trick (see Skill Box 28 on page 79), which helps him to get past Player A. Player A should not tackle Player B. Then it is the next player's turn.

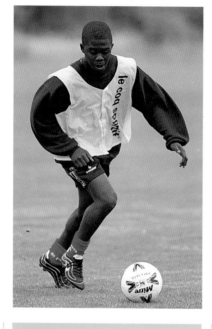

Drill 38
PROGRESSION A
Purpose: to practice dribbling improvisation under pressure
Players: 2
Level: intermediate to advanced
Equipment: ball

After practicing the move with no challenges, Player A attempts to tackle Player B when he tries his trick.

Drill 38
PROGRESSION B
Purpose: to practice dribbling improvisation and shooting
Players: 2
Level: intermediate to advanced
Equipment: marker cones, ball

Player B has to get past Player A and then shoot the ball into an empty goal, formed by two cones, 2 yards (2 meters) apart, 15 yards (14 meters) behind Player A.

Drill 38
PROGRESSION C
Purpose: to perfect dribbling tricks under pressure
Players: 3
Level: intermediate to advanced
Equipment: ball, full-size goal

The same drill as Progression B is performed with a full-size goal and a goalkeeper in position 25 yards (23 meters) behind Player A.

DRILL 39
THE PRESSURE DRILL

Purpose: to practice dribbling and trying to get past an opponent with the ball
Players: 2
Level: intermediate to advanced
Equipment: marker cones, ball

Set up a 20 x 10-yard (18 x 9-meter) grid divided into two halves. Put two cones, 1 yard (1 meter) apart, at the corners of the far side of the grid, the opponent's half. Player A receives the ball from Player B in his own half. He runs with the ball into his opponent's half and Player B tries to tackle him. Player A tries to dribble past his opponent, to either the left or the right, and if successful he passes the ball into the "goal" in the corner.

DRILL 40
PASS A PLAYER

Purpose: to practice dribbling and tackling skills
Players: 2
Level: intermediate to advanced
Equipment: marker cones, ball

This drill practices both dribbling and tackling. It is very demanding physically, since it requires nonstop running, so the drill should last for only three minutes before the different players are swapped in.

Set up a 20 x 10-yard (18 x 9-meter) grid with markers, setting up two small goals, marked with cones, 2 yards (2 meters) apart, at each baseline.

Player A sets off from his goal with the ball at his feet. His object is to dribble past Player B, using whatever tricks he can, and put the ball between the cones.

Player B starts off in his goal and must try to gain possession and score himself.

Drill 40
PROGRESSION
Purpose: to improve dribbling skills
Players: 2
Level: advanced
Equipment: marker cones, ball

A large part of the skill of passing a defender is committing him to a tackle, then winning the ball. The attacking player must tempt his opponent to go for the ball, to force a tackle while maintaining complete control.

Repeat the basic drill, but instruct the attacking player to let the ball go further away from his feet than before (though keeping it under control) to try and commit his opponent. Once the defender has missed the tackle he will be out of the game and the forward player will have space to attack.

▼ John Oster of Sunderland takes on his man in an English Premier League match.

chapter six

MAKING THE SAVE

Behind every great team there's a great goalkeeper. Goalkeepers have a reputation for being a little crazy, but in many ways they are the most important players on the field. A good goalkeeper can be the difference between a successful and a losing team. The importance of a reliable goalkeeper should not be underestimated. It's not just the ability to rescue a desperate situation with a split-second moment of brilliance. If you've got a goalkeeper who is calm, decisive, and clean in his kicking and handling, it brings confidence and security to the whole defense.

In the modern game, since the back-pass law was introduced, the goalkeeper has become the last outfield player as well as the last line of defense, meaning that the variety of skills and training routines needed to produce and maintain such a crucial all-around performer is huge.

The role of goalkeeper is the most specialized role on the field, which is why keepers need to train as much as, if not more than, other players.

DAVID SEAMAN

England star David Seaman may not be the most
flamboyant of goalkeepers — you won't see him charging
forward for last-minute corners or trying to dribble the
ball at the edge of his box — but that is exactly why
defenders appreciate having him behind them. They
know that when a cross comes into the box he'll deal
with it; when he needs to come off his line to kick, he'll
be there; and when the team is hanging on for a win in
the final seconds of a match, he'll make gravity-defying
saves to earn his team the points.

DRILL 41
CLAIMING CROSSES

Purpose: to practice jumping for and catching the ball from corners and crosses
Level: beginner to advanced
Players: 2
Equipment: full-size goal, ball

Having the confidence to come off your line and claim crosses in a crowded penalty area is one of the most important skills you must possess as a goalkeeper.

Player A plays crosses into the penalty area to a lone goalkeeper from in and around the corner flag. The keeper should stand toward the back of his goal 1 yard (1 meter) or two off his line. The crucial thing is that he should claim each cross at the highest point possible. Because of the extra reach of his arms, if he does this then no striker will ever out-jump him to the ball.

The keeper should be on his toes at all times, and as the ball is delivered into the box he should come forward from the back of his goal, using this momentum to get a good spring for his jump. He must learn to attack the ball decisively, extending his arms in mid-flight to claim it and then holding on tight and gathering the ball into his body.

SKILL BOX 29

THE "W" GRIP When catching the ball above your head, in front of your face, or to your side — from either a cross or a shot — to ensure a solid grip, your hands should be spread in the "W" position. This ensures the tightest grip and guards against the ball slipping through your fingers.

DRILL 42
CLAIMING CROSSES UNDER PRESSURE

Purpose: to practice dealing with crosses in a crowded penalty box
Players: 3 to 18
Level: beginner to advanced
Equipment: full-size goal, 5 balls

Dealing with crosses when there's no one in the penalty area is one thing, but when there are bodies everywhere and big, tall strikers challenging for the ball it's something else altogether.

In this drill Player A plays in crosses to the goalkeeper, Player B, with one attacker, Player C, challenging for the ball. Despite the presence of an opponent challenging for the ball, Player B, with his extra reach, should always be able to make the catch.

Slowly build up the exercise, adding more attackers and defenders until the penalty area is really crowded. The goalkeeper should call loudly for the ball so that his defenders know that he's coming for it and keep his eyes on the ball at all times. The key to success is for the goalkeeper to be positive and confident.

DRILL 43
PUNCHING

Purpose: to practice punching the ball clear when catching is impossible
Players: 6
Level: intermediate to advanced
Equipment: full-size goal, 5 balls

Sometimes, when the penalty area is extremely crowded and the goalkeeper has no clear run at the ball, it is safest for him to elect to punch the ball rather than catch it.

Two defenders, Players A and B, and two attackers, Players C and D, should be positioned around the near post. Player E should cross the ball to the near-post area from the corner flag. Because the goalkeeper's (Player F) run is blocked, he must use the extra reach of his arms to meet the ball at the highest point possible and punch it clear.

A goalkeeper has to decide whether to use a one- or two-handed punch. The two-handed punch is generally the safer option as you make contact with a larger area of the ball, however using one hand does give more reach.

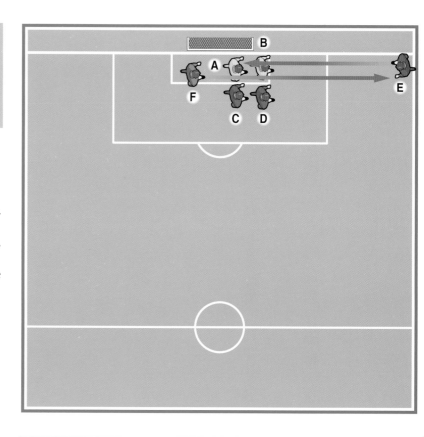

SKILL BOX 30

PUNCHING To give maximum control the goalkeeper's punch should be a short, sharp jab. You should bring your arm (if the situation allows, it should be your stronger arm as long as it is clear from any physical obstructions) back just 6 to 12 inches (15 to 30 centimeters) or so and execute a hard, firm punch, meeting the ball cleanly and squarely with your fist. If you swing wildly at the ball you will have no control and the ball may spin off anywhere unintended.

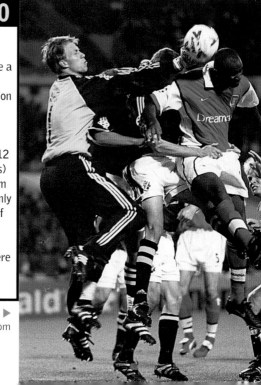

Mattias Asper, AIK Solna ▶ goalkeeper, under pressure from an Arsenal attack.

DRILL 44
CLINICAL KICKING

SKILL BOX 31

GOALKEEPER'S KICKING The important thing to remember when kicking a moving ball in a pressure situation is that you must make good, solid contact with the ball and clear it from the danger area. If the ball is coming hard and fast or at an awkward height, it may be best to sidefoot it away, using the inside of the foot for more control, and ensure good, safe contact. If a striker is bearing down on you, it may well be safest to kick the ball wide and into touch rather than to kick the ball straight forward, only to watch it ricochet off your opponent. Always keep your eye on the ball and your head steady, and make sure that your body position and stance give you a stable base from which to make a good, solid kick.

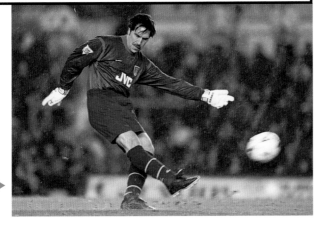

England's David ▶
Seaman kicks to
safety.

Purpose: to practice clearing the ball safely from a backpass
Players: 2
Level: beginner to advanced
Equipment: full-size goal, ball

Defenders must know that they can rely on their goalkeeper to deal with backpasses with his feet. As well as taking part in five-a-side and full games in training to improve their ball control, goalkeepers should practice their kicking during every training session.

From the edge of the penalty area Player A should kick the ball toward the goalkeeper, who must kick the ball straight back up the field, first time. The goalkeeper must get used to kicking the ball long and hard up the field, getting as much height and distance on it as possible. Player A should play some balls along the ground, some at waist height, and others that bounce in front of the keeper so that he gets used to dealing with all types of ball delivery.

Blackburn Rover's goalkeeper John Filan ▼
goes for distance.

DRILL 44
PROGRESSION A
Purpose: to practice clearing the ball to safety under pressure
Players: 3 to 4
Level: intermediate to advanced
Equipment: ball

The set-up for this exercise is the same as for the basic drill except that one or two opposing players run at the goalkeeper to pressure him as he deals with the ball.

Player A plays the ball in from the edge of the area as before and, as soon as the ball is kicked, Player B (who can start from any point behind the ball) runs at the keeper. Again, the ball should be played in at varying heights, angles, and speeds.

DRILL 44
PROGRESSION B
Purpose: to build upon ball-clearing skills
Players: 3
Level: intermediate to advanced
Equipment: ball

Player A, a defender, plays the ball back to the goalkeeper as he is being chased by Player B, an opposing forward. As Player B continues his run, Player A must move wide to make an angle for the goalkeeper, giving him the option of passing the ball back to him rather than kicking it long. This can be a very good way of retaining possession in a difficult game situation.

DRILL 45
DISTRIBUTION

Purpose: to practice locating teammates quickly with accurate kicks or throws
Players: 4 to 7
Level: beginner to advanced
Equipment: full-size goal, 5 balls

Goalkeepers are defensive players, but with clever, quick, and accurate passes they can often turn defense into attack.

In this drill Players A, B, and C stand in the "D" on the edge of the penalty area. Player A shoots toward goal and the goalkeeper should try to save the shot. If he does, Players B and C immediately spread out, making themselves available for a kick or throw from the keeper. Depending upon how many players are taking part in the drill, some can go wide to the edge of the box, others race

▼ Tony Bullock of Barnsley, England, gets the ball on the move.

upfield. The keeper must find a teammate immediately with a kick (full volley or half-volley) or throw (overarm for accuracy and distance, underarm for accuracy over short distances).

This routine is also very good for training outfield players to make themselves available when their keeper has the ball. A thrown ball is usually easier for an attacking player to control and, if executed properly, usually means that the goalkeeper's team retain possession. However, for a quick counterattack when the opposition defense is out of position, a long kick down the middle is preferable. During this drill all these tactical options can be replicated, teaching the goalkeeper to make the pass to the right player at the right time.

DRILL 46
AGILITY

Goalkeepers must always be on their toes — literally. It is crucial for them to be moving along their line and around their penalty area all the time, watching the ball and making sure that they are always in the best position to react to any situation.

For this drill place 20 markers in a line, 1 foot (30 centimeters) apart, then another 20 next to them but not directly opposite. The players (this is good for all players, not just goalkeepers) must run along the line stepping in the narrow gaps between the markers. To do this they have to move their feet very quickly and stay on their toes.

COACH'S TIP

Make the drill more competitive. Set up two lines of cones and two sets of players can race in a relay. This is a good way of ensuring that players move their feet as fast as possible. Any player who touches any of the markers must go back to the begining and start again.

DRILL 47
HANDLING WARM-UP

Purpose: to improve and maintain handling skills
Players: 2
Level: beginner to advanced
Equipment: ball, full-size goal

There is nothing more disheartening for a hard-working defense than to see their goalkeeper let a relatively simple shot or cross slip from his hands and an opposing striker score an easy goal. Handling, then, is something that goalkeepers should practice all the time.

From about 8 yards (7 meters) Player A kicks the ball at the goalkeeper, who is standing in his goal. Player A should start with easy balls for the keeper to grasp, then slowly make them more difficult. This drill should be done at the beginning of training sessions and, particularly, at the beginning of matches to give the keeper a "feel" for the ball.

DRILL 48
ON THE DECK

Purpose: to improve and maintain handling agility
Players: 2
Level: intermediate to advanced
Equipment: ball

The goalkeeper lies on the ground with the ball in his hands but with his back slightly raised. He throws the ball to Player A, who is standing at his feet, and in the same movement sits up. Player A throws the ball back at catching height, either above or to the left or right of the keeper. The keeper catches it, throws it back, and then rises to meet the next ball.

SKILL BOX 32

HOLDING THE BALL There's a great deal of difference between catching the ball and holding on to it, especially when there are goal-hungry strikers around. It is crucial after making a catch for keepers to gather the ball into their body. If you're on the ground, lie on top of the ball and gather it to your chest. If you're standing up, pull it into your chest and stoop down over the ball to protect it.

DRILL 49
THE REFLEX WALL

Purpose: to sharpen reflexes, athleticism, and shot-stopping
Players: 2 to 6
Level: beginner to advanced
Equipment: wall, 5 balls

Goalkeepers are expected to be solid and reliable, but what really sets great keepers apart is their ability to make breathtaking reflex saves. Reflex saves are partly instinctive, but goalkeepers work tirelessly in training to have the sharpness to get a hand to the ball when a goal seems certain.

At a distance of 4 yards (4 meters), the goalkeeper stands facing a wall. One or more players stand 6 yards (5 meters) behind the goalkeeper and drop volley balls past him at various heights and from various angles.

The goalkeeper has to stop the balls from going past him once they've bounced off the wall. Because he has his back turned, he hardly has any time to judge the angle and speed of the ball, hence his reflexes must be lightning fast.

If there isn't a suitable wall to use, the goalkeeper can stand in his goal with his back to the player or players, who stand 10 yards (9 meters) away. They drop volley balls, trying to score, but as they make contact they shout "turn." The keeper jumps around on his line and so has just an instant to react to the oncoming shot.

DRILL 50
BENCH BALL

Purpose: to improve and maintain reflexes and shot-stopping skills
Players: 2
Level: intermediate to advanced
Equipment: full-size goal, 2 workout benches, 5 balls

Place the benches at right angles to each other at the far post, as if making an arrow pointing toward the sideline. The goalkeeper must stay on his line while a player fires the ball low and hard at the benches from a wide position, varying where he aims for. Depending on where the ball hits and on which bench, it will ricochet either toward the goal or low and hard across it.

Every ball will come off at a different angle and the goalkeeper must stop it, testing his reflexes and shot- and cross-stopping abilities to the fullest.

**DRILL 50
PROGRESSION**
Purpose: to further improve and maintain reflexes and shot-stopping skills
Players: 2 to 3
Level: intermediate to advanced
Equipment: full-size goal, 2 workout benches, 5 balls

One or two strikers stand on the edge of the six-yard box so that when the ball ricochets across the box the keeper has to get back across his goal to face a shot if he can't clear the cross right away.

DRILL 51
RIGHT-ANGLING

Purpose: to practice narrowing the angle and shot-stopping
Players: 3 to 20
Level: beginner to advanced
Equipment: full-size goal, ball

Player A stands on the edge of the penalty area with his back to goal. Player B stands on the edge of the "D" just outside the penalty area.

Player B plays the ball forward through Player A's legs. As soon as it is through his legs, Player A turns and shoots first time. The goalkeeper must start on his line but as soon as Player B plays the ball he can race out to narrow the angle and make the target smaller by spreading his arms and standing tall. As soon as the keeper saves the shot or a goal is scored, he must make his way back to his goalline and the next two players take their turn.

SKILL BOX   33

NARROWING THE ANGLE In dangerous situations where strikers are in and around the penalty area and readying to shoot, or when they have a clean line to goal, you must come out and narrow the angle. That means coming forward off your line (not too far, otherwise the ball could be played over your head) so that the striker has the smallest possible sight of goal.

▲ Narrowing the angle against Arsenal in England's Premier League.

SKILL BOX   34

STAYING BIG In one-on-one situations you should physically try to make yourself a barrier between the ball and the goal by spreading your arms and standing tall, making the goal as small a target as possible. Be careful to stay on your toes and not to open your legs too wide, however, as a good striker will sometimes try to slot the ball through your legs and into the net.

DRILL 52
ONE-ON-ONE

Purpose: to practice narrowing the angle and shot-stopping
Players: 11
Level: beginner to advanced
Equipment: full-size goal, 10 balls

In a one-on-one situation when a striker has a clear path to goal it is crucial for any goalkeeper — if he wants to be the hero of the team — to narrow the angle that the striker has to aim at and to stay on his feet as long as possible (see Skill Box 33 on page 96).

Ten players line up 30 to 35 yards (27 to 32 meters) outside the penalty area, five on the right side of the field and five on the left. The goalkeeper must be on his line.

On the sound of a whistle, Player A runs with the ball toward goal and has five seconds to score. He may try to shoot from a distance or he may try to get around the keeper. As soon as the keeper touches the ball, a goal is scored, or if the five seconds are up, the ball is dead and the keeper must run back to his line. As soon as he gets there the whistle blows again and Player B (from the other side of the field) goes for goal. Repeat this pattern until every player involved in the drill has had a turn.

chapter seven

SET-PLAY PRECISION

A set play is a move that has been pre-arranged from a dead ball situation — a throw-in, corner, or free kick. When two teams are evenly matched, it is often a goal scored from a set play that ends up deciding the match.

The most dangerous set play is the free kick from outside the box — free-kick specialists can score one in three times within 30 yards (27 meters). Their skill is in beating the defensive wall, by curving the ball around them, curving it over them, a combination of both, or by hitting the ball so hard that they want to get out of the way. Then he has to beat the keeper.

Corners are also extremely dangerous if a team has a player adept at getting the ball into the box with curving corners and also players capable of heading or volleying the ball into the net.

The throw-in can also initiate a goal, particularly if a player in the team is able to throw the ball with some force into the penalty box, in which case a throw becomes almost as good to a team as a corner.

Set plays lend themselves to drills because they need to be practiced and practiced until they are perfected. They can also be used tactically to work out interesting ways of creating danger in the opposition goal.

DAVID BECKHAM

England's David Beckham is fast becoming known as the most deadly set-play expert in the world. His corners are incredibly dangerous as they swing into the box, as demonstrated in the 1999 European Cup Final when Manchester United scored twice from his restarts against Bayern Munich . And his free kicks from outside the box — curled delicately or hit with venom past the keeper — are very likely to result in a goal.

Beckham's technique is almost perfect, but he admits that he would not be nearly as effective if he didn't spend hours on the training field perfecting his craft.

DRILL 53
THE INSWINGING CORNER

Purpose: to practice the delivery of an inswinging corner
Players: 2
Level: beginner to advanced
Equipment: full-size goal, marker cones or a corner flag, 10 balls

Inswinging corners create maximum confusion for the defense because, if they are hit accurately, the goalkeeper is unlikely to come out to collect them, yet they finish up near enough to the goal to be easy to head in if the right contact is made. The more swing produced, the more dangerous the corner.

The more players who can take corners the better, so it's a good idea for everybody to practice the technique. It's best done in a real situation (with a goal and the corners marked out). If this isn't possible, recreate the situation by making a goal with cones and the corner marked out approximately 35 yards (32 meters) away.

Player A should try to curve the ball around a marker placed halfway between himself and the goal, 6 yards (5 meters) out from the sideline. He should try to swing the ball around the marker, so it arrives at head height at the

SKILL BOX   35

TAKING AN INSWINGING CORNER If you are right-footed you will take an inswinging corner from the left side (as you look toward your opponents' goal) and vice versa. To achieve the inswing, you will be aiming to strike the ball on the right edge. This will give the ball spin, curving it out and then in. To also help you add spin, take a starting run from the side of the ball (the left as you look at it). Keep your eyes on the ball and aim to strike it low down and on the right side with the instep of your foot. Keep your head down, lean back very slightly to give the ball some lift, and follow through with your kicking leg.

penalty spot. Player B should stand on the far post to either collect the ball and throw it back or head it into the back of the net. As the player becomes more proficient the marker should be moved further from the goal, 1 foot (30 centimeters) at a time, until it becomes impossible to swing the ball around it.

DRILL 54
THE OUTSWINGING CORNER

Purpose: to practice the delivery of an outswinging corner
Players: 2
Level: beginner to advanced
Equipment: full-size goal, marker cones or a corner flag, 10 balls

The outswinging corner, which curls away from the keeper, can be as dangerous as the inswinging corner. Any good coach knows that the more variety of corners that a team is capable of playing the more dangerous their attack will be.

Player A should repeat the inswinging corner drill, but try to swerve the ball inside the marker, rather than outside it, again trying to make the ball arrive at Player B standing just behind the penalty spot. Move the marker gradually inward from 5 yards (5 meters) out to develop the swing.

SKILL BOX 36

HITTING AN OUTSWINGING CORNER The technique involved in hitting a successful outswinging corner is identical to that of the inswinging corner. If a right-footed player takes a corner from the right instead of the left, hitting the ball in the same way as mentioned in Skill Box 35 (see page 100), the curve on the ball that makes it swing in when hit from the left is reversed — curving it out and away from the goalkeeper.

DRILL 55
ATTACKING THE FAR POST

Purpose: to develop the skills of taking an inswinging corner, heading, and timing runs
Players: 5
Level: intermediate to advanced
Equipment: full-size goal, 10 balls

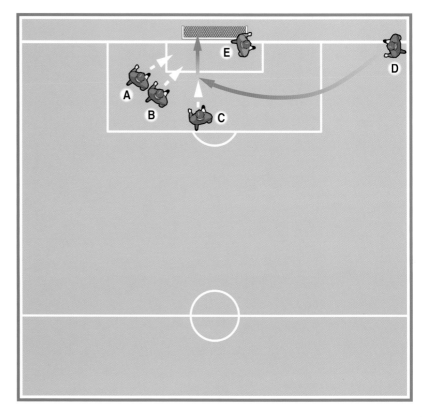

Once a player has mastered inswinging corners, it is important to start practicing them within a more realistic game situation, with attackers waiting to head in the ball and a goalkeeper attempting to catch or punch the cross away.

Players A and B stand on the edge of the far side of the box and Player C stands 5 yards (5 meters) outside the box (in the center of the field), and instructs Player D to take corners. In match situations, the three attackers should be the best headers of the ball in a team. However, whether they are defenders or attackers it is important for everyone to practice this skill. A goalkeeper, Player E, should be in position.

Players A, B, and C must time their runs toward the goal so that they start running as the corner taker is about to hit the ball. Practice the corners until they result in headers or volleys on target at least once every two corners.

DRILL 55
PROGRESSION

Purpose: to develop attacking and defensive awareness from corners
Players: 8
Level: intermediate to advanced
Equipment: full-size goal, 10 balls

Put three defenders (Players F, G, and H) into the box to make the attackers' job more difficult. Repeat the process with the outswinging corner. The more this drill is practiced, the more dangerous the corners will become.

For David Beckham precision is the key. ▼

DRILL 56
ATTACKING THE NEAR-POST CORNER

Purpose: to practice and improve taking an inswinging corner, heading, volleying, and timing runs
Players: 5
Level: intermediate to advanced
Equipment: full-size goal, 10 balls

Player A takes inswinging corners, aiming just above head height at a tall player (Player B) who is standing, facing the corner taker, between the line of the six-yard box, 5 yards (5 meters) from the sideline. The object of this exercise is for Player B to backhead the ball (see Skill Box 22 on page 61) into the box, and for players C, D, and E to run in from the edge of the box to attack the ball and head or volley for goal. The unpredictable flight of the ball after being headed by Player A will give the attackers the advantage over the defenders.

DRILL 57
THE UNEXPECTED VOLLEY

Purpose: to improve and practice taking inswinging/outswinging corners, and volleying and half-volleying skills
Players: 4
Level: advanced
Equipment: full-size goal, 10 balls

Player A is positioned on the edge of the penalty box, on the side of the "D" nearest the corner taker. Position Players B and C as if the corner were going to be hit toward the far post. Player D takes the corner and aims a low, hard ball so that it travels about 1 yard (1 meter) in front of Player A, who then hits it on the volley or half-volley (see Skill Box 6 on page 28).

In a match situation, often the opposing team will not think that Player A is in a threatening position and he will not be tightly marked. If this is the case, then players can elect to use the move practiced in this drill to attempt to score a goal from an unexpected volley.

◀ Dwight Yorke shows off some of his more unconventional shooting skills.

DRILL 58
THE DUMMY RUN

Purpose: to practice scoring headed goals from corners
Players: 4
Level: intermediate to advanced
Equipment: full-size goal, ball

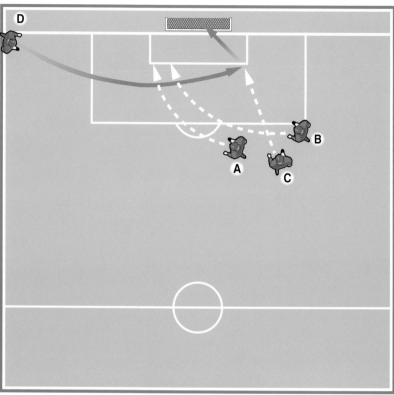

Position two tall players, A and B, on the edge of the box, with a smaller player, C, who is good at heading the ball, 10 yards (9 meters) or so behind them.

When the corner taker (Player D) is taking his starting run to kick an inswinging corner, Players A and B run diagonally across the box to the near post. Player C should then attempt to meet the ball at the far post with a header and score a goal. In a real match situation it is likely that, as Players A and B move, they will draw their markers with them, which will hopefully leave Player C free to score.

DRILL 58
PROGRESSION
Purpose: to practice scoring headed goals in a realistic situation
Players: 7
Level: intermediate to advanced
Equipment: full-size goal, ball

As players perfect the movements of this drill, three defenders can be introduced to make it more realistic for the attackers who will have to really think about their position.

SKILL BOX 37

INVENTING SIGNALS It is important with set plays that every team member know what is going to happen. The simplest way of doing this is to attribute a hand signal to every routine. Before taking a corner kick you could hold up your arm or put your hands on your head to denote a certain type of corner. It is best to make the system simple as players need to be concentrating on the task at hand rather than trying to remember a complex system of signals.

DRILL 59
LONG AND SHORT THROWS

Purpose: to practice taking throw-ins
Players: 3
Level: beginner to intermediate
Equipment: ball

It is important to practice both short and long throws in this drill. It can be done in two ways. Player A throws the ball to Player B, who then throws it back. Alternatively, Player A throws the ball to Player B, who after each throw moves back a few paces so that each player has to throw the ball greater distances. Player C checks for foul throws and makes the throwers do a forfeit (for example five push-ups) if they make a mistake.

SKILL BOX 38

THE THROW-IN A long throw-in can be as good as a corner, so it is a good idea for several players in one team to be able to put distance on their throws. As upper-body strength is important some extra gym work may be necessary.

A throw-in must be taken with both feet on the ground. The ball must be thrown from both hands, with the ball starting its trajectory from behind the head. Hold the ball firmly, with your hands forming a "W" shape, with the thumbs touching. To take a throw-in from a standing position, plant your feet firmly on the ground with your toes pointing outward. Hold the ball above your head, making sure your hands are in the correct position, and bend backward so your head and shoulders drop back slightly. Then straighten your back, moving your shoulders and arms forward, and let go when your arms are at their highest point. This type of throw is usually employed when the ball is needed to travel only a short distance.

To add more momentum to a throw to allow the ball to travel further, take a couple of paces forward, putting your weight on your front foot as you throw the ball, making sure that your back foot is touching the ground at all times. Most foul throws are caused by the back foot leaving the ground and some officials look out for this infringement scrupulously. You must also make sure that your feet don't go over the sideline.

DRILL 60
PASS BACK

Purpose: to practice passing the ball back to the thrower after a throw-in
Players: 2
Level: beginner to intermediate
Equipment: ball

The thrower is rarely marked by an opposing player, so one way of keeping possession from a throw-in is to pass the ball directly back to him. He can use the time he has before a player closes down on him to make a run with the ball or deliver a pass or cross.

Player A throws the ball to Player B, who is standing 8 yards (7 meters) away. Player B either controls it and passes it back to him or — even better because it will give the thrower more time on the ball when he gets it back — sidefoot-volleys or half-volleys it.

DRILL 61
THROWING DOWN THE LINE

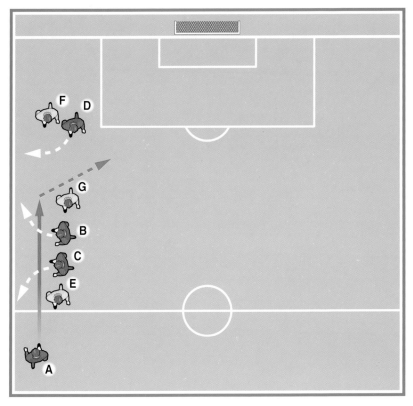

Purpose: to practice taking throw-ins down the line
Players: 7
Level: beginner to intermediate
Equipment: ball

If a team gets a throw-in deep in their own half, the safest way of getting it out of the danger area is throwing it "down the line." The player throws the ball as parallel to the sideline as he can, where a receiving player backheads it, controls it and turns, or passes it to another player.

Essentially the technique used is the same as for a long throw. Player A throws the ball to one of three teammates (players B, C, and D), who make runs near the sideline. Three opponents (E, F, and G) try to steal the ball.

Lazio's Juan Sebastian Veron eases ▼ the ball down the sideline.

DRILL 62
FREE KICK

Purpose: to practice and improve taking accurate, powerful, direct free kicks
Players: 5 to 7
Level: intermediate to advanced
Equipment: full-size goal, 20 balls

The Italian striker Gianfranco Zola and the English midfielder David Beckham have strike rates of one goal out of three free kicks outside the area. This is because they have practiced their craft to near-perfection, each man spending hours after training working on the accuracy, bend, and power of his shots.

Practice taking free kicks at goal from different central positions in the area from 30 yards (27 meters) out to the edge of the box. Form a three-, four-, or five-man wall, using taller players at each end. The keeper should position the wall to block off one side of the goal while he protects the other. Practice curling the ball around the wall or dipping it over the wall into the unprotected area. Alternatively, use a power shot to blast the ball past (or even through) the wall.

COACH'S TIPS
- Consider purchasing or creating a false wall made up of mannequins or cardboard cut-outs so the free-kick takers can practice the skill on their own.
- The most difficult shot to save is the one that goes in the top corners of the net. Tie a rubber tire to the crossbar on a short piece of rope so that it hangs just under the crossbar in the corner of the goal, and get the free-kick taker to practice aiming at the tire. This is how David Beckham practices his deadly accuracy.

Christian Ziege curves a free kick ▼
around the defensive wall.

SKILL BOX 39

THE SWERVING, DIPPING FREE KICK Kick the ball as you would with an inswinging corner but add top spin by raising your foot slightly as you curl it around the ball. This will make the ball rise, then dip as it curls around the defensive wall. If this is executed perfectly it is virtually impossible for the goalkeeper to make a save, but it is an extremely difficult skill to master.

chapter eight

DEFENDING THE LINES

Defenders may not get the glory of the striker or the creative midfielder, but their role in the team is just as crucial and the skills required just as tough to acquire and important to practice. A last-minute challenge, goalline clearance, or a well-drilled offside trap can be just as important as a stunning goal. Defending is not a one-person job and players must practice working together as a collective unit as well as honing their individual skills.

A good defender needs to be multifaceted. He needs to be able to tackle an attacker who is ready to use every trick in the book. He needs to be able to jockey a player from a dangerous position to an innocuous one without touching the ball. He needs to be able to head the ball clear of danger wherever it's come from. He needs to be able to read the game to anticipate the movements of the attackers he is trying to nullify. He needs to be able to trap and control the ball like a forward and pass it like a midfielder. He needs to be fast and strong.

The following drills are designed to improve the defensive capability of a team as a whole and each player individually. In the modern game every player needs to be a good defender, even the attackers. Remember, when a team doesn't have the ball, defense is the best means of attack.

PAOLO MALDINI

It's a tough one to call, but many professional observers rate Italy's Paolo Maldini the best defender in the world. Maldini, who can play at left-back or in the center of defense, has everything a defender needs. He is a wonderful tackler, has great ball control, is good in the air and, above all, his reading of the game is second to none. The fact that he is always in the right place at the right time is no coincidence: it's down to his brilliant positional sense and anticipation of the play going on around him.

DRILL 63
DEFENSIVE HEADING

Purpose: to improve defensive heading
Players: 2
Level: intermediate to advanced
Equipment: ball

The key to beating a player in the air is to move into position early, time the jump, and concentrate on the ball and not the other player or players.

Player A throws the ball, underarm, up in the air toward a defender, Player B, who is standing 10 yards (9 meters) away. Player B has to run toward the ball and head it at the highest point possible, back toward Player A.

Purpose: to practice defensive heading under pressure
Players: 3
Level: intermediate to advanced
Equipment: ball

In a match situation there will be very few occasions where a defender has a "free header." He is always likely to be under pressure from an opponent as they challenge for the ball too.

To build upon the basic drill introduce another player, Player C. He should be positioned halfway between Players A and B. This player's job is to challenge for the ball and make it harder for Player B to win the header. Player B should still steal the ball because he has a 5-yard (5-meter) starting run, which should give him the momentum to out-jump his opponent. Player C must be extremely careful not to foul his opponent — he must win the ball cleanly.

DRILL 64
CLEARING THE BALL

Purpose: to practice the skill of clearing the ball defensively
Players: 2
Level: intermediate to advanced
Equipment: ball

While it is true that defenders should generally aim not just to win the ball but to retain possession of it for their team, in dangerous situations in and around the penalty area often the sensible thing to do is to clear the ball to safety — either as far and wide up the field as possible or into touch, enabling the team to regroup.

This drill is designed to improve and maintain defenders' ability to clear difficult balls from dangerous areas: high balls, bouncing balls, low, hard balls that zip off the turf.

Player A stands 10 yards (9 meters) outside the penalty area and proceeds to play balls into the area at varying heights, angles, and speeds. Concentrate particularly on volleys and half-volleys, since these are the kinds of balls that are hardest to bring down, control, and pass to a teammate, and therefore it is often safest to kick them straight away from danger. The defender, Player B, must deal with each ball, kicking it back up the field or out of play.

SKILL BOX   40

SIDEFOOT VOLLEY When volleying a tricky ball clear of a crowded penalty area it is often safest to use a sidefoot volley. By making contact with the inside of your foot rather than the laces of your shoe you get more control over how and where you strike the ball. In a pressurized defensive situation, a mis-shot or sliced volley can result in giving possession of the ball straight back to the opposing team, but playing a sidefoot volley minimizes the risk of this.

◀ Kevin Muscat and Bob Taylor challenge for the ball in England's Division One.

DRILL 64
PROGRESSION
Purpose: to practice working as a defensive unit
Players: 5 to 6
Level: intermediate to advanced
Equipment: ball

Practice the same drill but position three or four defenders in the box. This will ensure that the defenders have to communicate with each other to decide which of them will go for the ball.

DRILL 65
BLOCK TACKLING

Purpose: to practice safe and effective block tackling
Players: 2
Level: intermediate to advanced
Equipment: marker cones, ball

Create two lines of cones to form a "tunnel" 4 yards (4 meters) long and 2 yards (2 meters) wide. Player A runs with the ball from one end; Player B comes from the other end to intercept with a block tackle. Remember that tackling carries a possibility of injury so you've got to get it right. This is a training drill so caution should be exercised. Tackling requires concentration, correct body movement, and commitment to the challenge. A player who goes in half-heartedly or without getting his body weight behind him is likely to get injured.

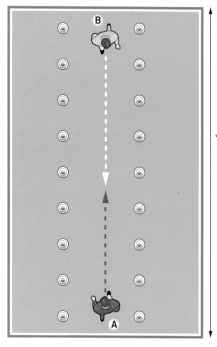

2 yards (2 meters)

4 yards (3.5 meters)

SKILL BOX   41

THE BLOCK TACKLE To execute a block tackle, concentrate on the ball but be aware of the movement of your opponent's feet and body. It is crucial that you choose the right moment to pounce. The best time is if your opponent looks up for a split second to weigh up his options. Just be sure that when you go for the ball you are going to make contact with it, otherwise you'll end up giving away a free kick or fall over as your opponent races past with the ball at his feet.

With a block tackle you are confronting your opponent head-on so you're going to have to go in strongly but fairly, with the inside of your foot, to steal the ball. Don't lean back as you go in for the ball; lean forward so that your body weight is over your tackling knee and taking the strain.

You may not come away with the ball every time, but if you get it right you should at least put a stop to the other team's momentum and hope that one of your teammates is on hand to pick up the pieces.

Manchester United's Jaap Stam ▶ demonstrates the perfect slide tackle.

DRILL 66
SLIDE TACKLING

Purpose: to practice safe and effective slide tackling
Players: 2
Level: intermediate to advanced
Equipment: marker cones, ball

The slide tackle is more of a last-ditch method of defense than the block tackle. It's highly risky because getting it right is difficult, and if you get it wrong you'll probably concede a free kick or a penalty, be in trouble with the referee, or your opponent will get a goal.

This drill must be supervised carefully and practiced safely. Remember that this is a training exercise and no player should attempt a tackle unless he is certain he is in a position to steal the ball. It is also important to practice the drill on soft grass, not on a hard surface.

Players A and B stand side by side, 2 yards (2 meters) apart. Player A has the ball. On the sound of a whistle both players run forward, and it is Player B's task to get into a position where he can slide in from the side, going down on his back, and push the ball away with his outstretched leg.

SKILL BOX   42

SLIDE TACKLE When attempting a slide tackle you must be aware of the rules of the game. Basically if you are deemed to have tackled a player from behind it is considered a serious foul and if officials apply the letter of the law you could be ejected — even if you have taken the ball cleanly. The message is clear: always make sure you are level with or in front of your opponent before attempting the slide tackle.

DRILL 67
JOCKEYING

Purpose: to practice defensive jockeying of an attacking player
Players: 2
Level: beginner to advanced
Equipment: ball

One of the most important aspects of defending is one of the least obvious skills in the game: simply standing up and jockeying an opponent so that he has nowhere to go or is forced to move to a less dangerous area of play (and his progress forward is slowed or stopped).

Often defenders will assume that if there is a player running at them with the ball they must attempt a tackle, but often it is much safer to stand up, back to goal if necessary (although always running side-on, in front of the attacking player but in the same direction as him while always concentrating on the ball), and make the opposition player do something really special to get past.

Player A has the ball at his feet and runs toward Player B, who backs away, staying on his feet, jockeying, and forming a barrier. The players should then swap roles.

SKILL BOX   43

JOCKEYING When jockeying an attacking player, you must weigh up the tactical situation and decide where on the field you are going to try to force him to go. By positioning your body to either the left or right of the oncoming ball you can effectively force the attacking player to go whichever way you want — so if you block the route to his left then he must go to the right. This is called "showing him inside" or "showing him outside."

For example, if there are a number of tall defenders who are good aerial players in the penalty box, the best option would be to try to force the attacking player wide so that the only thing he will be able to do is deliver a cross, which the defense should be able to deal with.

DRILL 68
MAN-TO-MAN MOVEMENT

Purpose: to practice man marking, intercepting, keeping possession, and closing down on an opponent
Players: 16
Level: intermediate to advanced
Equipment: marker cones, ball

As well as being an excellent drill for sharpening defensive skills, this is also very good for practicing ball control in tight areas.

Much of defending has very little to do with where the ball is and everything to do with where the attackers are — in other words, marking. Staying close to an

◀ Diego Simeone stays close to Andrei Shevchenko in Italy's Serie A.

attacking player wherever he goes, making sure he doesn't lose you and find the space he needs to receive a pass and create a goal-scoring opportunity, is a valuable skill all of its own.

Set up an area of 20-by-20 yards (18-by-18 meters) with two cones placed 2 feet (60 centimeters) apart in each corner. Divide the 16 players into two teams of eight. Four from each side are positioned within the square and the rest stand around the edge (two players from each side should stand between the cones).

The players play four against four. Team A (shown in blue) starts with the ball and tries to keep possession. Team B (shown in yellow) should try to close them down and man-mark all of their opponents so that the player from Team A who has the ball has no one to pass to. The object of the exercise is to pass the ball through either of the cone "goals." When this happens the players around the edge of the square play the ball to Team B and the drill resumes, this time with Team A trying to win possession of the ball. If the ball goes out of play the players around the edge of the square pass it back in to their teammates.

Each four-versus-four session should last no longer than five minutes, because this drill is both physically and mentally demanding.

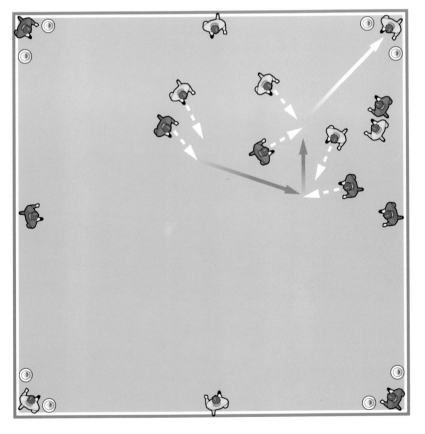

chapter nine

TEAMWORK

Even if a squad has some of the best individual players in the world, if they don't work together then they won't be a good team. Soccer is a team game — everybody must be able to work as part of a unit with one thought in mind: winning.

Teamwork is the ability of each individual to understand exactly what every other team member is doing and why. It is the ability to predict what your teammates will do because you know them so well: what runs they will embark on, what passes they will make. A team is a machine and teamwork is the lubricant that allows the machine to function smoothly.

Teamwork is also a mental attitude. A team has to stick together, and must not argue. It is the coach's job to raise and keep up the morale of a team, but it is every team member's responsibility to co-operate as much as possible.

The way to develop team spirit and to understand the capabilities and limitations of teammates is by playing together, match after match. However, a good deal can be achieved on the training field, if the sessions are undertaken with the right attitude.

The training drills in this chapter will test the teamwork of the players in your squad. They are specifically designed to help players understand that soccer isn't a showcase for individual talent — it is truly a team game.

FRANCE

In the 1998 World Cup competition France won the tournament as hosts, displaying superb teamwork to beat the Brazilians, whose game was based more on the individual brilliance of their players. France were a team without a recognized world-class striker but their teamwork helped them to overcome this problem, with goals coming from all positions, a fact underlined when their full-back, Lilian Thuram, scored both their goals in the semifinal against Croatia.

USA

The USA's monumental World Cup win in front of more than 90,000 fans in June 1999 was a triumph of teamwork. It was collective spirit, determination, and tactics as much as individual skill and ability that drove them on in the ferocious heat of the Pasadena Rose Bowl. Playing against an equally well-organized and driven Chinese team, the US side maintained its defensive discipline with Kristine Lilly's goal-saving header on the line typifying the team spirit. When it came to the mental toughness required in a penalty shoot-out, with Brandi Chastain smashing home the winning kick, proving they were up to the task.

DRILL 69
PUSH IT OUT

Purpose: to practice defending as a unit and squeezing the play
Players: 7
Level: intermediate to advanced
Equipment: full-size field, ball

The key to successful defending is positioning. Players must be aware of where their teammates are. A crucial job of any defense is to push up the field when their team has possession, squeezing the play so that if the opposing side gains possession of the ball they have very little space to play in.

This simple drill allows a defense to practice pushing up and squeezing the play. It is vital that a defense moves together when a team pushes forward. If one player is slow to come out he can play an attacker way over on the other side of the field onside and leave him clean through on goal.

Two attackers, Players A and B, play against four defenders, players C, D, E, and F, and a goalkeeper, (Player G). The attackers should be encouraged to shoot for goal. As soon as the situation arises where the goalkeeper has the ball, on the command of one of the central defenders, the entire defense should form a line and move up the field. The defenders should listen to the instructions of whoever is calling the line, moving up the field as far as he orders but always staying in a straight line.

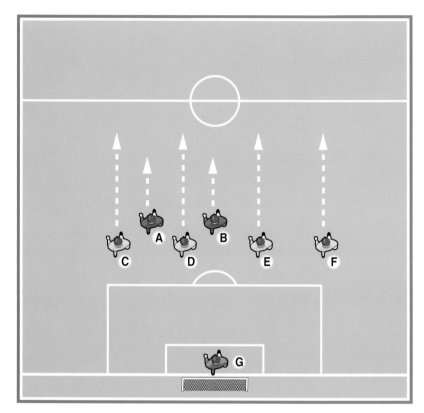

Ronaldo tries to beat his Moroccan ▶ rivals to the ball.

DRILL 70
OFFSIDE

Purpose: to practice playing an offside trap
Players: 7
Level: intermediate to advanced
Equipment: full-size field, 5 balls

If a defense is well-disciplined and the defenders work together and communicate well with each other, a team can take pushing up and squeezing the play a step further by trying to employ an offside trap. This can be particularly effective at goal kicks and long kicks from the opposition keeper when, on a certain call, the entire defense can step forward at the right moment and catch opposing strikers offside.

This drill involves going through the routine of setting an offside trap at walking pace. Usually an offside trap would be played by four defenders (A, B, C, and D), and they should line up on or behind the halfway line. Level with them will be the two strikers (Players E and F), anticipating a long ball over the top.

At a given moment—for instance when the goalkeeper makes the first movement of his drop kick—the four defenders take a step back. One of the central defenders should work out a specific call to instruct his teammates to do this.

As soon as they have stepped back, and just before the ball is actually kicked, the defenders should step forward again three or four times. Hopefully, as the defense has stepped back, the forwards will have gone with them, leaving them offside at the instant the ball is kicked and the

defenders have stepped back up the field.

Once players have mastered the drill at walking speed, they should try doing it at full pace.

DRILL 70 PROGRESSION A
Purpose: to practice playing an offside trap at a realistic speed
Players: 10
Level: intermediate to advanced
Equipment: full-size field, 5 balls

The four defenders (A, B, C, and D) stand in a line, marking players E and F on the edge of the center circle. Player G has the ball on the other side of the center circle.

The defenders are in line with the two attackers. When they see that Player G is about to kick the ball they all move up in line, hoping to catch the two attackers offside when the ball is played. It is important that they raise their hands to appeal for offside as soon as the ball is kicked—and that they are ready to chase back if the decision isn't given.

Two other players should act as referees to make the decision as to whether or not players are offside.

DRILL 70 PROGRESSION B
Purpose: to practice defending as a unit and holding the line
Players: 7
Level: advanced
Equipment: half a full-size field, 5 balls

This drill combines playing an offside trap with pushing up and squeezing the play.

Four defenders (A, B, C, D) play against three attackers (E, F, and G). The attackers start with the ball in the center circle and try to break down the defense as the defenders attempt to hold their line straight and steady and push up the field to make it hard for their opponents to move and pass the ball.

At intervals throughout the drill all of the players should stop and stand exactly where they are and assess their position in relation to their teammates and the opposition. This way each player can learn very quickly what he is doing wrong. The defenders will become well drilled in holding a line and knowing where on the field that line should be, depending upon where the ball is.

DEFEND AND ATTACK

Purpose: to develop all-around offensive and defensive teamwork and technical skills, and increase and maintain fitness levels
Players: 18
Level: intermediate to advanced
Equipment: half a full-size field, 2 full-size goals, marker cones, 10 balls

England defender Sol Campbell often ▶ makes attacking runs.

These games should be played in a competitive spirit to try to reflect what happens in a real match situation.

Use cones running from the edges of the 18-yard box to the halfway line and cones going across halfway up to create a halfway line. Set up a portable full-size goal on the halfway line.

The drill involves two teams, A (shown in yellow) and B (shown in blue), each with nine players made up of three defenders, three attackers, two wingers, and a goalkeeper. Three attacking players and three defensive players are stationed in each half. The attackers are supported by two wingers, each of whom stands between the markers and the real sideline. The goalkeepers stand in the goals.

The ball is played onto the field and the game commences. The attackers must try to score any way they can, either by interpassing and dribbling or by passing out to the wingers and trying to hit their subsequent crosses past the goalkeeper. The defenders try to stop them and launch the ball into the other half. The wingers cannot go beyond the markers running parallel to the sideline.

Once the game starts, no players can move out of the half they are stationed in. This will help players improve their positional sense.

DRILL 71 PROGRESSION
Purpose: to strengthen offensive and defensive teamwork, and further increase fitness levels
Players: 30
Level: intermediate to advanced
Equipment: half a full-size field, 2 full-size goals, marker cones, 10 balls

Introduce 12 more players, half representing one team, half representing the other. They should be lined up alternately along the sideline running from the 18-yard box. These players are not allowed to tackle or score, but they can receive wall passes from their teammates.

The players should swap roles after three minutes.

DRILL 72
COUNTERATTACKING

Purpose: to teach and practice quick counterattacking teamwork
Players: 11
Level: intermediate to advanced
Equipment: full-size field, full-size goal, 10 balls

As soccer teams at all levels get more and more organized and defenses get harder and harder to break down, swift counterattacking has become a more crucial weapon in a team's armory. Often the only time that there is enough space to create goal-scoring opportunities is when one team has pushed forward on the attack but the other has regained possession and swiftly and incisively moved the ball back up the field to catch its opponents on the break.

Teams that are good at this usually have fast strikers and players with the ability to play the ball forward, accurately at speed, between each other while moving fast themselves. If they are going to capitalize on the instant when their opponents are at their most vulnerable then they must literally turn defense into attack in a matter of seconds. There can be no delaying on the ball, no weighing up options.

This drill is played in one half of a full-size field and encourages attacking players to be quick and incisive in attack as soon as they gain possession. It encourages urgency and directness in play, with attacking players playing at a speed that tests defenders.

Line up a defensive team, Team A (shown in yellow — four defenders, two midfielders, and a goalkeeper), against an attacking one, Team B (shown in blue — four attacking players). Team A starts with the ball. They must play it around while Team B tries to close down on them and win possession.

As soon as they do so, Team B has 10 seconds to get a shot on target. If after 10 seconds they have not managed an attempt on goal, Team A gets the ball back, and the exercise starts again.

The drill can be varied by giving more or less time to the attackers depending on ability levels. Try to reduce the time they are given as they improve.

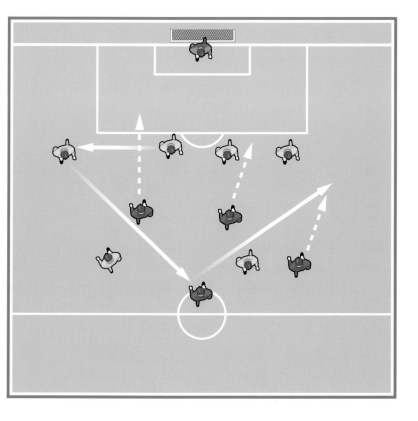

GLOSSARY

ATTACKER A player in a forward role whose main objective is to score goals and create scoring chances for others.

BACKPASS A pass from a player back to his own goalkeeper. The goalkeeper must kick a backpass unless the ball has been headed to him.

BY-LINE The line that runs along the top and bottom of the field.

CENTER CIRCLE Positioned at the center of the halfway line. At the kick-off, players from the side that do not have the ball must stay in their own half and outside this circle.

CHIP An airborne pass or shot. The ball is kicked while it is on the ground.

CORNER KICK A kicked ball from the point where the touchline meets the by-line, after the ball has gone out of play over the by-line with a defending player having touched it last.

CROSS A pass that is made from the side to the middle of the field, usually into the penalty area.

THE "D" Semi-circle at the edge of the penalty area. When a penalty is taken, all of the players, apart from the goalkeeper and the penalty taker, must be outside both the penalty area and the "D".

DEFENDER A player who generally plays close to his own team's goal, whose main objective is to prevent the opposition from scoring.

FOUL Any piece of play or incident on the pitch which contravenes the rules and regulations of the game.

FREE KICK A kick awarded to one team by the referee after foul play (or offside) by a member of the opposing team. The kick is taken where the offense took place and opponents must move at least 10 yards (9 meters) away.

GOAL A point-scoring play achieved when the ball legally crosses the goalline – under the crossbar and between the posts. The word is also used for the actual structure created by posts, crossbar, and a net that the ball must pass into.

GOALKEEPER The only player on the field who is allowed to use his hands to play the ball. He can move anywhere on the field but cannot handle the ball outside his team's penalty area.

GOAL KICK A kick to put the ball back into play from anywhere inside the six-yard box taken by a defending player or the goalkeeper after the ball has gone out of play over the by-line when an opposing player touched it last.

GOALLINE The line between the two posts of each goal. The whole ball must cross this line for a goal to be awarded.

HALFWAY LINE The line that divides the field equally into two halves, parallel with both by-lines.

HANDBALL Illegal playing of the ball with the hand or arm.

HEADER Playing of the ball with the head, usually the forehead.

KICK-OFF The play that starts the match, the second half, and the restart after a goal is scored (when it is taken by the team that has conceded the goal). Both teams must stay in their own half of the field for the kick-off, and the team that has the kick (decided by a toss of the coin at the start of the match) must play the ball forward.

LOB A lofted pass or shot, played when the ball is in the air.

MIDFIELDER A player who generally plays in the space between his team's attack and defense, combining the roles of attacker and defender.

OFFSIDE Complicated rule which states that the player furthest forward of the team that is attacking must be level with or behind the defender(s) (not including the goalkeeper) when the ball is played forward in the opposition half.

PASS An intentional ball played to a teammate.

PENALTY A direct shot on goal from 10 yards (9 meters), awarded for foul play in the penalty area.

PENALTY AREA A marked-out area (18 yards/16 meters out from the goal) at each end of a soccer field, in which goalkeeper can handle the ball, and fouls by the defensive team are punishable by a penalty kick.

PUNT A long kick upfield by a goalkeeper who drops the ball onto his foot from his hands.

SAVE A play made when a goalkeeper successfully intercepts a strike on goal.

SHOT A kick toward goal with the intention of scoring.

SIX-YARD box A marked out rectangle within the penalty area within which goal kicks can legally be taken.

THROW-IN An overhead throw, using both arms, from the touchline. Used to restart the match after the ball has gone out of play.

TOUCHLINE The line that runs along the two long sides of the field.

VOLLEY A kick where the foot makes contact with the ball while it is in the air.

WALL A voluntary line-up of defenders to protect their goal when the opposing team has a free kick. The players must be at least 10 yards (9 meters) from the ball.

USEFUL ADDRESSES

Associations

American Youth Soccer Organization
National Support & Training Center
12501 South Isis Avenue
Hawthorne, California 90250
Toll-Free 1-800-USA-AYSO
Tel/fax (310) 643-6455
http://www.soccer.org
National youth soccer organization that promotes open participation, balanced teams, positive coaching, and good sportsmanship.

Canadian Sport and Fitness Administration
Centre, Inc.
1600 James Naismith Drive, Suite 307
Gloucester, Ontario K1B 5N4
Tel (613) 748-5602
Fax (613) 748-5706
http://www.cdnsport.ca
Official home of National Sport and Active Living organizations in Canada.

Canadian Soccer Association
237 Metcalfe Street
Ottawa, Ontario K2P 1R2
Tel (613) 237-7678
Fax (613) 237-1516
E-mail <info@soccercan.ca>
http://www.canoe.ca/SoccerCanada/
Member of FIFA.

Canada's Sports Hall of Fame
Exhibition Place
Toronto, Ontario M6K 3C3
Tel (416) 260-6789
Fax (416) 260-9347
http://home.inforamp.net/~cshof/

Fédèration Internationale
de Football Association (FIFA)
FIFA House, Hitzigweg 11, P.O. Box 85
8030 Zurich, Switzerland
Tel 011-41-1-384-9595
Fax 011-41-1-384-9696
http://www.fifa.com
The governing body for international soccer, including the World Cup. The latest on rules, officiating, and all aspects of the game.

National Alliance for Youth Sports
2050 Vista Parkway
West Palm Beach, Florida 33411
Tel (561) 684-1141
Fas (561) 684-2546
http://www.nays.org
Non-profit advocate association for healthy, positive, and safe sports for children involved in out-of-school youth sports activities.

National Soccer Hall of Fame
Wright Soccer Campus, 18 Stadium Circle
Oneonta, New York 13820
Tel (607) 432-3351
Fax (607) 432-8429
http://www.soccerhall.org

Soccer Association for Youth
4050 Executive Park Drive, Suite 100
Cincinnati, Ohio 45241
Toll-Free 1-800-233-7291
Tel (513) 769-3800
Fax (513) 769-0500
E-mail <SAYUSA@soccer.org>
http://www.saysoccer.org/
A youth soccer organization that promotes safe, enjoyable, and fair competition.

Sport Canada
8th Floor, 15 Eddy Street
Hull, Quebec K1A 0M5
E-mail <sportcanada@pch.gc.ca>
Federal government branch supports the achievement of excellence in, and development of Canadian sport.

United Soccer Leagues
14497 North Dale Mabry, Suite 201
Tampa, Florida 33618
Tel (813) 963-3909
Fax (813) 963-3807
http://www.unitedsoccerleagues.com
The largest system of national soccer leagues.

United States Amateur Soccer Association
7800 River Road
North Bergen, New Jersey 07047
Toll-Free 1-800-867-2945
Fax (201) 861-6341
http://usaussf.com
Member of U.S. Soccer Federation and FIFA.

United States Soccer Federation
1801-1811 South Prairie Avenue
Chicago, Illinois 60616
http://www.us-soccer.com/
Member of FIFA.

United States Youth Soccer Association
899 Presidential Drive
Suite 117
Richardson, Texas 75081
Toll-Free 1-800-4-SOCCER
http://www.usysa.com/
Fifty-five non-profit and educational state associations across USA for youth at all ages and levels of competition.

Printed and on-line magazines

FIFA News; FIFA
FIFA, P.O. Box 85
CH-8030 Zurich, Switzerland
http://www.fifa.com/fifa/pub/index.magazine.html
Official publications of FIFA, published in English, French, Spanish, and German. Annual subscription rate is valid for both.

Fundamental Soccer
828 E. Portland
Fresno, California 93720
http://www.fundamentalsoccer.com
Interactive youth soccer on-line magazine.

Major League Soccer
110 East 42nd Street, 10th Floor
New York, New York 10017
Tel (212) 450-1200
Fax (212) 450-1300
http://www.mlsnet.com

La Cancha
http://www.lacancha.com
Popular on-line magazine.

Soccer
5211 South Washington Avenue
Titusville, Florida 32780-7315
Toll-Free 1-800-376-2237
Tel (407) 268-5010
Fax (407) 269-2025
http://www.soccerchallenge.net/soccermag/
Features on coaching, youth games, parenting, refereeing, events and championships, and the NCAA Final Four.

Soccer America
P.O. Box 23704
Oakland CA 94623
Toll-Free 1-800-335-GOAL
Fax (818) 760-4490
http://www.socceramerica.com

Soccer Digest
990 Grove Street
Evanston, Illinois 60201-4370
Tel (847) 491-6440
Fax (847) 491-0867
Top players, big games, team schedules, and stats.

Soccer Jr.
27 Unquowa Road
Fairfield, Connecticut 06430-5015
Tel (203) 259-5766
Fax (203) 256-1119
E-mail <soccerjrol@aol.com>
Focuses on players of the American Youth Soccer Organization.

Solo Soccer
6601 Tarmef Drove, Suite 100
Houston, Texas 77074-3634
Tel (713) 774-4652
Fax (713) 774-4666
Features international soccer reports, interviews, game reviews, and analysis.

Women's Soccer World
1728 Mulberry Street
Montgomery, Alabama 36106
Tel (334) 263-0080
Fax (334) 264-8129
http://www.womensoccer.com

INDEX

▲ Members of the under 21 squad. From left to right: Dave Collis, Pierre Bolangi, Sam Turner, Yohance Lewis, Alex Martin.

The publishers would like to thank personnel from Charlton Athletic FC, England, for allowing us to photograph their players and for generously giving their time and expertise.

Particular thanks go to:
Keith Peacock – First team coach
Gary Stevens – Under 21 coach

▲ Thanks to members of the Charlton Athletic Centre of Excellence (Female) and The Women's Football Academy of the South East (in partnership with Charlton Athletic Community Scheme and Bexley College).